»»» STOP BULLSHITTING YOURSELF »»»

>>>>>>>>>>>> **STOP BULLSH YO**

ITTING
URSELF >>>>>>>>>>>

DREW HANLEN

wm

WILLIAM MORROW
An Imprint of HarperCollins*Publishers*

STOP BULLSHITTING YOURSELF. Copyright © 2025 by Drew Hanlen. All rights reserved. Printed in the United States of America. No part of this book may be used or reproduced in any manner whatsoever without written permission except in the case of brief quotations embodied in critical articles and reviews. For information, address HarperCollins Publishers, 195 Broadway, New York, NY 10007.

HarperCollins books may be purchased for educational, business, or sales promotional use. For information, please email the Special Markets Department at SPsales@harpercollins.com.

Foreword by Jayson Tatum
Foreword by Joel Embiid

FIRST EDITION

Designed by Kyle O'Brien

Artwork by Raj Bhullar

Library of Congress Cataloging-in-Publication Data has been applied for.

ISBN 978-0-06-341335-1

24 25 26 27 28 LBC 5 4 3 2 1

CONTENTS

CONTENTS

FOREWORDS

I started working out with Drew when I was just thirteen years old. I'll never forget our first workout, because he tried to kill me. Drew thought I was too young to take on as a full-time client, so he put me through one of the toughest workouts I've ever done, just to test my mental toughness and to see if I would quit. Not going to lie, I had to leave the gym a few times to throw up, but I wasn't about to let him break me. At the end of that workout, Drew invited me back for another session the next day, and we've been working together ever since.

Being from St. Louis, I saw how much Drew helped Bradley Beal develop throughout high school and wanted to follow the same blueprint. I started working out at 6 A.M. every morning because that's what Drew and Brad both did to elevate their games. It wasn't easy waking up that early every morning, but it quickly became a routine I loved. While everyone else was still sleeping, I was grinding. By the time my classmates were showing up for school, I had already put in a ninety-minute workout. I wasn't going to let anyone outwork me.

During our first week of workouts, I started to see what Drew was all about. He started by having me work on different variations of jabs, over and over, perfecting the smallest details. We didn't even shoot a shot for the first few days. Most kids my age would have been bored out of their minds, but I loved it. I could feel the work translating from our workouts to the games, and it made me fall in love with the process. That's how we've always approached things: focusing on one skill at a time until it was mastered, then moving on to the next. We started with the mid-post, then mid-range, then off-the-dribble moves, and so on. We always had a blueprint for my career, and we attacked it piece by piece.

We still use that same process today. We're constantly breaking down my film and analytics, searching for ways to improve my game. The reason that we work so well together is because he's just as obsessed with my development as I am. He cares about every guy he works with and puts in the same effort we do. He's up early in the morning and late at night, always trying to find solutions to our problems and helping us be the best we can be.

Drew is more than a trainer—he's family. He's been there to celebrate my greatest moments and has helped me find my way through the toughest ones. Whether I'm in a slump or just in need of a confidence boost, Drew's always been there for me. He's also always challenging me to think bigger and to believe that I can be one of the greatest players of all time.

That's what this book is all about. It's about constantly evaluating your life and realizing that there's always another level. And to reach those new levels, you need a system. Drew's system has helped me and many of the top players in the world, and it can help you too.

Winning a championship was one of the best experiences in my life, but the real motivation comes from knowing that I can do it again. Because when the great ones get to the top of the mountain, they keep climbing.

—*Jayson Tatum*

• • •

When I saw Drew sitting courtside at a Summer League game in Las Vegas before my rookie season, I walked over, introduced myself and told him I wanted to work with him. I was already a fan of his, having watched his videos and seen how all his players improved. I knew he was the guy I needed to train with.

He was open to working together, but mentioned he was flying back to LA later that day. One thing I've learned is that you must take advantage of every opportunity you get, so I changed my travel plans and the very next day, I flew to LA for our first workout.

Growing up in Cameroon, basketball wasn't even a part of my life until I was a teenager. At sixteen, I had an opportunity to attend a basketball camp that would change my life—but I almost didn't go. I was so scared that I skipped the first day. When my dad found out, he basically forced me to go the next day, and that decision set me on a path that took me to America and eventually to the NBA.

But nothing about my journey has been easy. When I moved to the US, I didn't speak any English, and I was so bad in my first high school practice that my coach kicked me out of the gym. I remember crying in my dorm room, wanting to quit. The only thing that kept me going was how I was raised. My parents always taught me to push through, no matter how tough things got. Even though I sucked, I made myself show up to the gym every day, convinced that the hard work would eventually pay off.

Little by little I started improving, and eventually I accepted a scholarship to Kansas. Initially, I planned to redshirt, but I ended up playing and having a strong season—until it was cut short by injury. I missed the

NCAA tournament and declared for the draft, only to get sidelined again by another injury. As tough as the injuries were, they didn't compare to what happened next. I lost my brother and best friend, Arthur, when he was just thirteen. Losing him nearly broke me. I was in such a dark place, and all I wanted was to go home to Cameroon. There were a lot of rough days, but I knew quitting wasn't an option. I kept going because I knew Arthur would've wanted that for me and our family.

Two years later, after rehabbing relentlessly, I finally was healthy enough to work on my game again. That's why I was so eager to get in the gym with Drew. Since then, he's been a huge part of my journey, and working with him has been one of the best decisions I've ever made. He's more than just a coach—he's someone who believed in me before I even believed in myself and continues to challenge me to reach levels I never thought possible. Drew didn't just think I could be one of the best players in the league; he believed I could be one of the greatest of all time. Together, we've put in countless Unseen Hours—watching film, working on every aspect of my game, and building the mindset it takes to be the best.

And that's exactly what this book teaches you—the mindset, the system, and the strategies to push past what feels impossible. Just like he did with me, Drew shows how to overcome obstacles, eliminate doubts and excuses, and believe in yourself even when your goals seem out of reach. He's helped me reach levels I didn't think were possible, and he can help you too.

Everything I'd been through—the injuries, the heartache, the work—all felt worth it during the 2023 MVP ceremony. Being named the league's Most Valuable Player meant so much to me, not just because of the award, but because of the journey it represented. But the moment that will stay with me forever wasn't holding the trophy—it was holding my son, Arthur, as he ran across the court to hug me. In that moment, I knew I'd kept my promise—to never quit, to honor my family, and to make my brother proud.

—*Joel Embiid*

»»» STOP BULLSHITTING YOURSELF »»»

A WORD FROM DREW

If you picked up this book, it's because somewhere deep down, you know you've been bullshitting yourself. You know that making more money, landing a better job, and finally getting in great shape will make your life better. You're also aware that worrying and stressing less, eliminating anxious thoughts, getting rid of the pain from your past, and eliminating toxic relationships will improve your life as well.

But for some reason, you've settled.

You've read self-help books, listened to peak-performance podcasts, retweeted motivational quotes, attended yoga sessions, tried dieting and exercising, hired a therapist, and countless other remedies. But you still haven't found solutions to your biggest problems.

And so, the big question remains: What can you start doing to finally turn your life around?

The answer is to stop bullshitting yourself.

This book is a game plan for doing just that.

For the past seventeen years, I've helped many of the world's best basketball players reach levels that they didn't even think were attainable.

From winning gold medals, championships, and MVP and scoring titles to being selected to the All-Star and All-NBA teams, my clients continue to reimagine what is possible when you conquer self-deception and master your relationship with yourself.

Within these pages, you'll learn the system and strategies that have propelled them to success, and I'll teach you how to apply these same principles to every aspect of your life.

Whether you want to improve your game, your business, or your life, this book will provide you with an actionable blueprint to identify and confront the narratives, excuses, and obstacles that have held you back—so that you can finally achieve a level of personal and professional success that you may not even believe is possible.

THE
BULLSHIT

In 1963, the Bronx Zoo in New York City opened an exhibit titled "The Most Dangerous Animal in the World." Before it opened, people became increasingly curious to discover which animal had earned the title.

When they were finally allowed in, visitors hurried to THE MOST DANGEROUS ANIMAL IN THE WORLD sign that hung above what appeared to be a dimly lit, barred cage. When they looked through the bars, they encountered the most dangerous animal in the world—but not in the way they had expected.

Rather than a ferocious beast, they saw their own reflection in a mirror behind the bars, implying that they were the most dangerous animal. Visitors were stunned. Most expected to see a monster, but none of them expected to see themselves in a reflection.

One of the visitors spoke up, asking the question that was on everyone's mind: "What does this mean?" After a brief pause, an older man sitting quietly on a nearby bench said, "It means that the most dangerous animal is not out there. It's in here," while pointing to his head and his heart. "The greatest threats aren't the monsters that lurk among us, but rather the monsters that lurk within."

Fast-forward almost sixty years.

Early in the 2021 season, I was sitting courtside at a Sixers versus Celtics game in Boston, watching two of my NBA All-Star clients, Joel Embiid and Jayson Tatum, play against each other.

Jayson had a great game, but Joel finished 3 of 17 from the field and scored a season-low 13 points. We were twelve games into the season, and Joel was averaging 22 points per game, far below what he was capable of. After the game, he said, "I need you in Philly tonight."

Joel could have easily been okay with averaging 22 points per game, which would still rank him as the 17th-best scorer in the league. He could have easily coasted his way into another NBA All-Star game by also averaging 11 rebounds and 4 assists per game. And he could have easily not cared about his play since he had signed a $196 million contract just two months before that guaranteed him every penny regardless of how well he performed. He also could have blamed the double-teams and defensive schemes his opponents were throwing at him or the fact that he had an All-NBA teammate that was sitting out and refusing to play.

But excuses don't improve execution. And settling doesn't produce success. Joel knew he was capable of more and that he had the power to change his situation.

> EXCUSES DON'T IMPROVE EXECUTION.
> SETTLING DOESN'T PRODUCE SUCCESS.

I got to his home in Philly around 1 A.M. that night, and we immediately started breaking down film, talking through the smallest of details, and pinpointing how he could start elevating his play.

You might be curious why one of the best players in the world was up so late hunting for answers. Well, that's precisely what makes him one of the best in the world. He's obsessed with getting better and relentless in finding ways to improve his game.

We spent hours analyzing his film from the beginning of the season and comparing it to film from the best games of his career. Then we watched film of Michael Jordan, Shaquille O'Neal, and Kobe Bryant, three of the most dominant scoring threats of all time. We also watched film of Kevin Durant, Dirk Nowitzki, and Hakeem Olajuwon, whose play we've modeled parts of his game after. Joel was fully committed to finding solutions. I don't remember how much we slept that night, if at all, but I do remember us creating a blueprint we felt confident would work moving forward.

The Blueprint we collectively decided on was straightforward, as the best ones usually are. Dominating the paint needed to become a priority for Joel again, which meant more paint, post, and elbow touches, and more drives to the rim.

A few nights later, he put up 28 points, 12 rebounds, and 4 assists in a win against the Atlanta Hawks. More important, he felt more like himself on the court. In his next game against the Charlotte Hornets three days later, Joel exploded for 43 points, 15 rebounds, and 7 assists.

Joel was back.

His points from paint, post, and elbow touches and drives to the rim jumped from 13.3 to 22.6 points per game, igniting a run that ended with him as the NBA scoring champion, averaging 30.6 points per game.

SETTLING FOR LESS

Most of you are just like early-season Joel. You're doing fine but living far below what you are capable of. You're coasting through life with plenty of justifiable excuses to validate your shortcomings.

The problem is, unrealized potential eventually becomes pain. Sometimes it reveals itself almost immediately. Other times, the pain builds up inside of us over the years, and by the time we realize it, there's nothing we can do about it.

That pain is the direct result of not dealing with the bullshit in your life when you had the chance. You can't always avoid suffering, but you can minimize its impact by destroying bullshit thoughts, feelings, emotions, excuses, and actions that are holding you back or causing you to settle for less.

> YOU CAN'T ALWAYS AVOID SUFFERING, BUT YOU CAN MINIMIZE ITS IMPACT.

Like Joel, you have the power to change. The trick with eliminating your bullshit is believing you have the power to do it. Much of what is holding you back is the imaginary demons that live in your head. Slay those demons, and you kill the pain.

Take a second to imagine what your life might look like if you were doing everything you should be doing. What if you were eating and sleeping well, managing your stress, exercising, spending time with good people, avoiding drama and those who create it, and working with purpose on something that you enjoy doing? I bet your world would look a lot different and much better than it does now.

As kids, we were asked frequently what we wanted to be when we grew up. An astronaut? A ballplayer? A doctor? A ballerina? Those asking us were daring us to dream. The funny thing is I don't remember any of my grade school friends saying they wanted to be broke, lonely, stressed, anxious, insecure, or depressed. No one answered that they were going to work jobs they didn't like, feel stuck in unhealthy relationships that stress them out, or struggle financially.

Sadly, that's where many of us find ourselves–in a reality far from our ideal job, perfect partner, the mansions we saw on *MTV Cribs,* or the fairy-tale life we've always envisioned. The ironic thing is some of the people who do have the partner, house, or job that they once dreamed of having still feel lost, stuck, or un-fulfilled.

What's to blame for this mess?

You guessed it . . . the BULLSHIT!

And who's to blame for this mess?

You guessed it again . . . YOU!

Now, you might be wondering, "How did I get here?" but the more important question is "How do I break free from this cycle?"

Before you can figure that out, you must understand that bullshit is everywhere, and that your bullshit is different from my bullshit or anyone else's. Even people who appear to have it all figured out have some degree of bullshit in their lives. Chances are, they've just found ways to minimize it.

There are lots of steps involved in arriving at that place, but you can get there. The first step is figuring out what kinds of bullshit are in your life so you can confront them and start living a life that brings you inner peace and that you are proud of.

THE DEEP GAMES

The only way you can defeat the bullshit is by winning The Deep Games—the games that constantly take place deep inside your head and your heart. These are often battles you may not even know you're fighting. To win them, you're going to have to dig in and unravel all the bullshit you've allowed to remain in your life.

That sounds complicated because it usually is. You've got twenty, thirty, or forty years of bullshit to slay. That won't happen overnight, but eventually it will if you keep chipping away.

You can't will it away and POOF! the bullshit is gone. Oh, if only it was that easy. Getting rid of the bullshit demands genuine changes, backed by consistent efforts to overturn the bullshit that's been dragging you down for so long.

It's difficult, but I've helped some of the world's best athletes take on enormous challenges and win. I've also watched friends, family members, and others take on their own challenges and do the same, which means you can too.

PUTTING IT OFF

"Diet starts Monday."

Recognize those words? They're the famous last words you utter right before you decide to pig out and break the diet you promised that you would finally stick to.

You and everyone else know that the diet probably won't start on Monday and if it does, it will probably end on Tuesday, Wednesday, or soon after that. When you cheat and gorge before you even start, it's only a short matter of time before you again rationalize what you want in the moment (a Chick-fil-A chicken sandwich with waffle fries and a Cookies & Cream milkshake) over what you want in the long run (a healthier body and lifestyle).

Procrastination is just one of the many ways we bullshit ourselves. The problem is that you've become so good at this type of bullshitting that it's an ingrained part of what you do and who you are. You've become such a master at deflecting, delaying, and putting things off that it's second nature to you. Most of your stresses, struggles, and insecurities stem from procrastination bullshit.

Think about it . . .

You say you want to lose weight, but you refuse to improve your eating and workout habits. Perhaps you want to be in a healthy relationship, yet you refuse to dump your toxic partner. Or you long to spend more time with your family but continue to work too many hours at a job you generally hate.

I bet you're thinking, "I would make those changes, but . . ." Whatever follows "but" is bullshit unless you follow that "but" with "I don't want it bad enough."

It's not easy to eat healthy and exercise daily. I get that you don't want to leave or hurt the person you say you love. And I know finding a well-paying job with more reasonable hours isn't easy.

You can justify all the excuses in your head for whatever parts of your life where you're falling short. However, that kind of thinking does nothing for you. If you truly wanted to change, you would.

CONVERSATIONS WITH YOURSELF

"We need to talk" are four words that will cause your stomach to drop and head to spin.

When a parent, loved one, or best friend utters those

words, you know they have something serious to tell you. You immediately start preparing for a tough conversation because if it wasn't that serious, they would have just said what they needed without the warning. We hate these talks because they usually make us face harsh realities that we would rather avoid.

As self-deceit and bullshit gurus, we've mastered the art of beating around the bush, sugarcoating, and sweeping things under the rug, so we aren't fans of having uncomfortable conversations that force us to acknowledge and take responsibility for things we'd rather ignore.

I have news for you. Before someone else says, "We need to talk," you need to look in the mirror and say those exact words to yourself. The time for dodging and hiding from the one person who you ultimately can't bullshit ends now.

It's time to have the uncomfortable and honest conversations with yourself that you've been putting off the longest and are most afraid to have, because they are the exact ones you need the most. You must start with the biggest and most important things in your life. They're the ones that can produce the most change, and change is what you've got to do if you want to live a better life than you are now.

You're probably thinking, "I don't even know which

conversations to have," or "Nothing is really that bad in my life right now, so maybe I'll have that talk sometime down the road."

Bullshit! There is *always* something to work on that will make your life better.

Also, notice that I said "honest" conversations. Not "kind of honest" or "mostly honest," but 100 percent pure and unadulterated honest. The ones where you keep it real with yourself and don't tiptoe around the truth, no matter how much the truth hurts. Don't lie and end up feeling stupid after the fact because you think you outsmarted yourself by avoiding the hard work. All you did was waste time better spent searching for the truth. If lying isn't an indicator of how much work you have to do, then I don't know what is.

We hate when our family members or our friends lie. So why would you lie to the most important person in your life? In other words, why lie to yourself?

And if you're lying to yourself by saying that you never lie to yourself, just know that's the biggest lie of them all.

It's time to get real, which is going to require you to dig deep enough to uncover some unpleasant truths that you have been afraid to discover. While these conversations aren't fun, they provide the reality and gut check that are always necessary for growth and improvement.

Playing dumb and ignoring the bullshit in your life might make you feel better in the short-term, but it ends up killing you in the long run. When you don't take a cold, hard look at who you are and where you want to go, you'll live in ignorance.

Ignorance isn't bliss.

Ignorance is bullshit.

JUMPING TO CONCLUSIONS

As a trainer to some of the best players in the NBA, I've seen a lot of gravity-defying jumpers in my time. But that doesn't compare to the number of people I meet who are all-world at jumping to conclusions.

Don't believe me? Think about how you *actually* approach these events instead of how you *should* approach these events.

> Your spouse sends you a text that reads, "I have something to discuss with you when you get home."
>
> Your boss calls you into their office at the end of the day on Friday and closes the door behind you.
>
> Your doctor walks into an examination room and says, "I got your results back," followed by the longest pause of your entire life.

You couldn't help but make assumptions while reading these scenarios. Chances are your head filled with thoughts that each of them would turn out bad.

But what if your wife wanted to tell you she's secretly planned a romantic getaway for your upcoming anniversary because she loves you more than ever? Or better yet, that she is pregnant, and you'll soon become parents, which is what you've wanted for the past several years?

What if your boss called you in to offer you a promotion and a raise but wants to give you the weekend to enjoy the news privately with your family before announcing it to everyone the following Monday?

And how would you feel if your doctor said your cancer screening tests came back negative, and you're healthier than you've been in a long time?

You're probably thinking, "They should have just said those things instead of scaring me." The problem is they didn't do anything wrong. You did. You jumped to the wrong conclusion and made up a story in your head. That was *your* story, not *the* story.

You do things like this all the time because you've been trained to do things like this all the time. Through a lifetime of conditioned responses, you always assume the worst instead of imagining the possibilities of better outcomes. And you need to stop.

Maybe you cheated on an ex in the past and remember the hell you went through when they caught you, which is why your heart dropped when you got that text from your wife, even though you've been 100 percent faithful. Perhaps you were fired from a job late on a Friday afternoon, and you've felt vulnerable in the workplace ever since. Worse yet, while you got a great result at your doctor's this time around, that may have been preceded by a cancer diagnosis in the past.

These types of anxious thoughts are reflections of your biggest fears. Making matters worse, these situations, and many others like them, are outside your control. You're burning up emotional energy unnecessarily instead of accepting that some form of news is coming and adopting a wait-and-see attitude.

If you've been faithful to your wife, kicking ass at work, eating well, sleeping well, working out consistently, and taking care of your body, what is there to worry about? When you've done all that you can, accept outcomes as they happen, knowing you did the best you could.

On the other hand, if you've been neglecting your spouse, just going through the motions and coasting at work, or you've been slacking about your health, then you might be concerned with what's to come.

The point is, if you've done nothing wrong, assume nothing's wrong!

Since jumping to conclusions doesn't burn calories the same way jumping rope does, it's time to break that bad habit as quickly as you can, and you will start down a path of stopping some of the bullshit in your life.

TUNING OUT THE BULLSHIT

Every year since 2012, I've run the NBA pre-draft process for dozens of lottery picks, including multiple number-one-overall picks. The pre-draft process is the most intense and important time during a prospect's life, because it's a chance for them to improve on their weaknesses and add new skills that will potentially move them up the draft boards. Players usually lift weights, watch film, and go through two on-court workouts each day for two months to transform their body and game before they work out in front of scouts and front-office executives, who will decide what order they get selected on draft night.

In 2014, one of the players I helped was Zach LaVine. Zach only started one game for UCLA as a freshman, but he decided to leave school early to enter the NBA Draft. He was projected to be the twenty-ninth pick in part because scouts openly criticized his decision.

"Amazing to me that UCLA's Zach LaVine thinks he's ready for the NBA. He's not even a decent player," wrote one *Sports Illustrated* reporter.

"Zach LaVine would look really good in a Maine Red Claws uniform next season," added an ESPN scribe.

"Don't see how Zach LaVine is going to have an immediate impact in the NBA when he couldn't even have a major impact in the NCAA Tournament," said a CBS analyst.

I showed him mock drafts and these quotes on the first day we worked together and told him, "None of these guys have a pick. All of this is bullshit. Don't pay any attention to it."

New articles continued to pop up doubting Zach's ability to do well in the NBA. By this time, we knew what Zach's skill level was, and we dismissed each opinion as simply more bullshit. We kept laughing, tuned it out most of the time, and kept working.

Six weeks later, during his Pro Day, Zach was ready to show everyone how much he had improved. And he got to do it in front of more than 150 NBA decision-makers from every team in the league.

He shined in one of the most legendary Pro Day workouts of all time and jumped up the draft boards the next day. Ultimately, Zach was selected thirteenth by the Minnesota Timberwolves in the 2014 draft and has since become an NBA All-Star and a gold-medal-winning member of Team USA in the 2021 Olympics.

Zach's ability to tune out the bullshit is one reason he has become one of the most talented shooting guards in the NBA.

BREAKING FREE

The Truman Show is a movie starring Jim Carrey as Truman Burbank. He thinks he's living a boring life as a kindhearted insurance salesman. What Truman doesn't realize is that thousands of cleverly hidden cameras have been watching his every move for nearly three decades.

Truman's entire life is a simulation streamed as a reality TV show. He's unaware that he is living in an artificial world and doesn't realize he has the power to exit the simulation and leave the show at any time.

Sometimes it's hard to see how trapped you are until you are free.

In one scene, an angry fan of the show calls the producer to express frustrations about Truman being stuck in his "cell." The producer responds, "He could leave at any time. If his was more than just a vague ambition, if he was determined to discover the truth, there's no way we could prevent him. I think what distresses you, really, caller, is that ultimately Truman prefers his cell, as you call it."

SOMETIMES IT'S HARD TO SEE HOW TRAPPED YOU ARE UNTIL YOU ARE FREE.

Are you a Truman Burbank? If you knew you were living below what you're capable of, would you be determined enough to break out and go for it? If not, what's stopping you?

Here's another great line from the movie. "We accept the reality of the world with which we are presented."

Talk about a universal theme. That describes why so many people spend their lives working jobs they hate or staying in relationships that stress them out. They sheepishly accept the life they've been given instead of taking control and creating the life they want. Choosing to settle for a subpar version of what you believe you deserve, rather than rejecting those low standards, is bullshit.

Like Truman came to realize, sometimes the only thing that is stopping you from living the life you dream of is you.

THE HUMAN HUMANE SOCIETY

You've probably seen the Humane Society and ASPCA's heartbreaking commercials that show sad, lonely animals that have suffered from abuse, been abandoned, or need a home. After watching these ads, you can't help but feel for these animals, and oftentimes it makes you want to save one right away.

Let's pretend that the Humane Society rescued lonely, lost humans instead. We'd have overflowing shelters filled with people who need help. Unlike dogs, though, if you think you'd find yourself in one of those shelters, you don't have to wait for someone to come adopt you. You have the power to save yourself!

Life often tosses us in the deep end of the pool and drags us down with some added weights to test our ability to swim. Ideally, we can freestyle our way through life, but sooner or later, most people find themselves doggy paddling and just trying to keep their heads above water. Others are always treading water like hell to keep themselves afloat.

They haven't figured out that letting go of all the added weight they carry around will make the challenge of keeping their head above water a lot easier. Additionally, they haven't recognized that they hold the power to walk out of that shelter whenever they're willing to leave their past experiences behind.

If you sense that your life is more difficult than it ought to be, examine the extra weight you carry on your back. You might not be on the verge of drowning, or perhaps you're continually struggling to reach the surface for a breath of air, but swimming through life shouldn't be any tougher than it already is.

INTERNAL PEACE

I'm a big fan of the movie *White Men Can't Jump*. Woody Harrelson's character, Billy, is a trash-talking basketball player who is constantly betting on himself during pickup games and shooting contests.

There is a scene in the movie where his girlfriend, Gloria, threatens to leave him if he continues to gamble. Billy heads to the streetball courts anyway and ends up winning more than he's ever won before, only to come home to an empty apartment because Gloria packed up her stuff and left him. Billy has an "a-ha" moment, remembering what Gloria told him earlier:

"Sometimes when you win, you really lose. And sometimes when you lose, you really win."

This is a perfect analogy for life. No matter how much it looks like you're winning from the outside, if you're losing on the inside, you *are* losing.

> NO MATTER HOW MUCH IT LOOKS LIKE YOU'RE WINNING FROM THE OUTSIDE, IF YOU'RE LOSING ON THE INSIDE, YOU ARE LOSING.

You can appear to have it all on the outside while still feeling like shit on the inside.

Regardless how big your house is, how nice your cars are, how beautiful your partner is, how powerful your job title is, or how wealthy you are, you can still feel empty, lonely, anxious, and insecure. You can be on top of the world and still feel like the world is on top of you.

I know for a fact there are celebrities with millions of fans and piles of cash in the bank who go to sleep feeling lonelier and more broke than the fans that look up to them. What's the point of having millions of fans if you're not a fan of yourself?

Of course, you need money to survive. But you need peace to thrive.

The famous athletes and entrepreneurs I work with look like they live perfect lives from the outside. They have multiple cars, big houses, and fans who adore them while getting paid millions of dollars to play a game they've loved all their lives.

But they face the same problems as the rest of us on the inside. In fact, some of their problems are super-sized because they're always in the public eye. Through them, I've come to realize that true success isn't driven by external forces. Success is determined by how at peace you are with yourself.

When I coach players, this is a big part of the message I give them:

"Your peace isn't determined by how much money you have or all the other trappings of success. Your peace comes from knowing who you are, being comfortable with your shortcomings, and finding ways to use your gifts and talents beyond making your own life better. When your internal thoughts and feelings align with how you move about in the world, you will find that peace."

Billy learned a hard lesson when he lost Gloria. He won at one part of life, but that victory cost him something much more valuable.

If your life is not aligned with the right purposes and priorities, you'll feel empty even when you succeed. Be clear on what you want from life. You'll enjoy your successes more, and when you win, you'll truly win.

DENYING IS LYING

By now, I hope you're starting to identify all the types of bullshit in your life. If not, you're probably in denial. And you guessed it, denial is another type of bullshit.

Maybe you're in denial that you have a drinking problem, even though you consistently find yourself hungover every weekend.

Or you tell yourself you're over your ex even though you check their social media, look back at old photos on your iPhone, and "randomly" text them to check in, secretly hoping to rekindle what you once had.

Some of you tell yourself you're fine with your body even though you've put on fifty pounds, can't stand looking at yourself in the mirror, and will avoid shopping for new clothes at all costs because you're embarrassed.

Denial is a defense mechanism that eases temporary pain. That pain, left untreated, begins to fester and grow. It hurts more and causes a lasting pain that's harder to treat, just like any physical ailment that doesn't receive care as soon as it's diagnosed.

Denial is a horrible form of bullshit because you can't fix a problem until you believe there is a problem that needs to be fixed. And you can't resolve something that you refuse to acknowledge.

> YOU CAN'T FIX A PROBLEM UNTIL YOU BELIEVE THERE IS A PROBLEM THAT NEEDS TO BE FIXED.

When you're in a state of denial, the ironic thing is that you may be expending more energy to deny a problem and keep living with it, rather than facing it head-on. While it's true that you may burn more energy in the short-term, confronting the issue instead of denying it can ultimately save you valuable time and energy in the long run. And you won't have to keep dealing with the mental burden if you make up your mind to take care of business as soon as possible.

The journey through bullshit is shorter than the alternative path of denial around your bullshit.

There is no denying we all have bullshit. No one is perfect. And that's okay! Inner peace isn't about pretending we are bulletproof. Instead, it's about properly handling everything on our plate, including all the unwanted stress and struggles that come our way.

You don't get points for how tough you may appear. You get points for how at peace you actually are.

THE BLAME GAME

If I had you list all the problems in your life, you'd probably forget to add your name to that list. Yet, you created most of the problems that you're experiencing right now. That may be a tough pill to swallow, but it's true.

I'm sure you'd rather blame your situation on anything else. But pointing the finger at anyone other than the person in the mirror doesn't solve anything. There are a ton of people who came from messed-up families and situations a lot worse than yours who are out there thriving because they found ways past the pain.

If you're like most people, you place blame on your parents, your partner, your friends, your circumstances, and your past traumas. While all of those people and things played a part in who you are today, it's time to take ownership of the role you played in all this and figure out ways to get past whatever has been holding you down.

Others may have caused you pain, but you're not going to allow them to continue to hurt you. You can't go back to fix what's already happened, so you have to accept where you're at now and realize that you have the power to rise above any challenges that are thrown at you moving forward.

It's time to let go of the bullshit, drop the excuses, and start realizing it's up to you to take responsibility and control of your life. You have the power to change and heal. And the power to move forward and turn your life around. You've played victim far too long. You're not stuck, lost, or out of hope.

You're just bullshitting yourself.

Regardless of which excuses fit your narrative, you must decide you're no longer going to justify the bullshit.

BEING GOOD TO YOURSELF ISN'T SELFISH

Growing up, I heard a lot about the Golden Rule.

Do unto others as you would have them do unto you.

Nowadays, some self-help gurus call upon the Platinum Rule instead.

Do unto others as they would want to be done to them.

Two rules teaching us how to treat others, yet no rules teaching us how to treat ourselves?

It's actually amazing how little we take care of ourselves. We often sacrifice our own well-being to live up to the selfless rules of putting others first. We tell ourselves we're leading a good, virtuous life when we do.

> THE GOLDEN RULE TEACHES US HOW TO TREAT OTHERS, BUT WE NEED TO LEARN HOW TO TREAT OURSELVES.

The problem is that this comes at the expense of taking care of us more than it should. I'm all for being good to others, but you also must make sure you're being great to yourself. After all, the most important relationship in your life is the one you have with yourself.

> THE MOST IMPORTANT RELATIONSHIP IN YOUR LIFE IS THE ONE YOU HAVE WITH YOURSELF.

Not being good to yourself is bullshit.

I started to realize how little people prioritize their well-being when CEOs started hiring me to help them get their lives together. They devoted the entirety of their day to putting out fires while allowing the flames of their personal challenges to rage unchecked.

In our first meetings, I'd always ask, "If someone you loved needed your help, would you help them?" and with no hesitation, they all said, "Of course."

I'd smile and respond, "Well, someone you love needs your help. And that someone is you."

It was the quickest, most honest, and effective way I knew to get through to them. It only took ten seconds but I opened the door wide to help them stop their bullshit.

GO BAKE YOUR CAKE

I had a college professor who would always say, "Go bake your cake." The first few times she said it, everyone just shrugged it off. But after a while, one of my classmates finally asked, "Why do you always say that?"

She explained that it was a saying she stole from her grandma and then told this story.

Grams had a sign in her kitchen that read, PEOPLE PRAY FOR CAKE. THEN WHEN GOD GIVES THEM FLOUR, EGGS, OIL, ICING, A PAN, AND AN OVEN, THEY GET FRUSTRATED AND LEAVE THE KITCHEN. So anytime y'all tell me your aspirations or business ideas, I tell you to "Go bake your cake" because you have everything you need to get exactly what you want, but you have to be willing to put in the work to get it.

Years later, when I think about that day in class, the message hits even harder. Life doesn't always give you exactly what you want. But it does give you plenty of ingredients to bake something special out of it.

And yes, I hear the bullshit creeping in: "Some people have better ingredients, better appliances, better kitchens, blah blah blah."

So what? They're simply baking a different cake than you. Forget other people's ingredients. What's stopping you from baking your cake?

Are you lazy? I hope not because being lazy is disrespectful to all the people who have sacrificed and believe in you.

Are you afraid to fail, so you choose to play it safe? Playing it safe is the most dangerous thing you can do. When you try to protect yourself from failure, emotional pain, or disappointment, you become your own worst enemy.

Or is it that you refuse to take ownership for your part in not having the things you want in life? That means you've made a choice to blame your circumstances, partner, boss, parents, upbringing, or whatever has kept you from your dreams.

Excuses are rationalizations. They're the voices inside our heads that tell us we're doing okay even when we've been kicked hard. Excuses are bullshit. Set them aside.

Go bake your cake.

I know you have it in you because I've seen people from way tougher backgrounds, who were raised by more-messed-up families, pull through and handle even worse stuff than what you're going through. Once they put aside their excuses and added the right ingredients to their lives, they started living the kind of life you deserve to live as well.

I'm not downplaying what you're currently dealing with, where you came from, or what you've been through, but it's time to take back control of your life. It's time to defeat whatever bullshit is keeping you out of the kitchen.

Let me show you how.

THE AUDIT

Being able to identify bullshit in general is big.

Being able to identify *your* bullshit is bigger.

Whether you realize it or not, one of your biggest problems is that you aren't always able to identify your real problems.

When someone else is overweight, you can easily point to their eating habits or lack of exercise as the problem. If your friend or relative is constantly in a bad mood or stressed out, you usually know it stems from their draining relationship or their shitty job. It's easy to see their problems, even when they can't.

Yet, when you're dealing with those exact same issues, you blame your body struggles on your genetics and pretend that your relationship or job is going to magically improve one day.

Why is it so easy to spot the bullshit in others' lives, and so hard to spot our own? It's because we're self-deceit gurus who have mastered the art of making up stories, justifiable excuses, and rational reasons to make us feel better about our shortcomings.

If you really want to identify the bullshit in your life, you have to stop the surface-level sugarcoating. You must dig deeper to have the uncomfortable conversations with yourself that you know you need to have but are afraid to. While those conversations universally suck, they are the ones you need if you want to take back control of your life.

Taking ownership of the bullshit you uncover and coming to terms with you being in control of your life is yet another uncomfortable realization for a lot of people. It's easier to blame their situation or others for all their stresses, struggles, shortcomings, and insecurities.

Self-improvement starts with defeating your bullshit. And the only way to defeat the bullshit in your life is to first identify which kinds of bullshit exist.

The Audit will help you understand where you're at now, how the past is still playing a big role in your life, and where you want to go in the future.

Unless you suffer from eisoptrophobia (I'll save you a Google search: it means an extreme fear of mirrors), I'm guessing you look at yourself in the mirror every morning.

But when was the last time you took a thorough look at your life? When was the last time you took time to evaluate everything in your world, internally and externally?

You have the ability to create the life you want instead of accepting the life you think you're stuck with. But to do that, you have to know why and where you are by analyzing the present and how you got here by looking at your past. You must also give thought to where you want to get to in the future and what you need to do to get there by shrinking the gap.

> *YOU HAVE THE ABILITY TO CREATE THE LIFE YOU WANT INSTEAD OF ACCEPTING THE LIFE YOU THINK YOU'RE STUCK WITH.*

Then, you have to put together a blueprint to get there, do the work, and make adjustments and improvements along the way so you can finally enjoy the life you're capable of living.

WINNING WITH THE CARDS YOU'VE BEEN DEALT

It's time to get REALLY honest with yourself. You are the reason you're killing it or not.

You are exactly where you are in life because of the actions and decisions you've made to this point. If you're not where you want to be, you may want to point to your many excuses for what's holding you back. As we've already covered, you probably don't realize you're the one holding on to the bullshit that's holding you back and weighing you down.

I understand that you don't get to pick your parents, siblings, race, genetics, the neighborhood you grew up in, or the financial situation you're born into. But you get to decide how to move forward to make the best of each of those conditions. I also get that some hands are easier to win with than others, but the dealer doesn't always give us the cards we want.

If we could control our circumstances, I promise you that as a basketball junkie who dreamed of playing in the NBA, I would not have asked to be a 5'11" white guy with average athleticism.

Like me, you play the cards you've been dealt. The good news is that in poker and in life, every hand has the potential to be a winner if you play it the right way. Your challenge is to take the best actions to improve your chances of winning.

> *EVERY HAND HAS THE POTENTIAL TO BE A WINNER IF YOU PLAY IT THE RIGHT WAY.*

Worrying or wishing for a better hand does nothing. Working to win with the hand you were dealt does everything. I'm empathetic to the challenges people face, but regardless of how messed-up or unfair the environment you grew up in was, you must shift your focus toward solutions—both in the present and for the future—to overcome those difficulties.

What you do today and from this day forward means more than any day you've already lived. Some people like to justify their shortcomings by convincing others that they've had it worse than most. They're only bullshitting themselves, trapped in a victim mentality.

The truth is there are plenty of people who grew up in poverty and are now incredibly wealthy. There are others who had to overcome parents who were on drugs, or who were victims of domestic violence or major crimes. Despite significant obstacles of all kinds, people who succeeded refused to accept that a bad hand was a losing hand. They played the cards they were dealt and turned those hands into winners.

These people didn't use others as an excuse. They didn't blame race, physical limitations, a poor education, or a broken home life. They controlled what they could, which were their decisions and actions, to overcome a deck that was stacked against them.

Accepting your hand is the most critical piece of your audit. If you don't face reality, you can't play the cards you've been dealt and win.

AUDITING YOUR DECISIONS AND ACTIONS

You are where you are because of your decisions and actions to this point. Owning your decisions and actions, good and bad, is an essential step to stop bullshitting yourself.

For better . . .

If you're a high school athlete and get a college scholarship, it isn't because you had one great game. It's because of the years of hard work and sacrifices that made you talented enough for college coaches to want you as part of their program.

When you get a promotion at your job, it isn't because you had one great day at work. It's because you've been kicking ass and getting results for a long time.

Those times you look in the mirror and see six-pack abs aren't because you had a salad for lunch and rode the Peloton for an hour three times this week. It's because you've been eating healthy and putting in hard work at the gym for months.

For worse . . .

For those of you in a less-than-ideal marriage, it isn't because you woke up and randomly decided you were no longer right for each other. It's because you've ignored and overlooked all the warning signs, even though they were obvious to everyone else for a long time.

If you feel like you don't have any friends, it isn't

because all your friends held a meeting one morning and decided to collectively walk out of your life. It's because you pushed away the friends you had and didn't welcome in new ones.

When you struggle financially, it isn't because somebody robbed you. It's because you haven't made enough money to live the life you think you deserve, or you haven't been smart enough with the money you made.

Your past decisions and actions have led you to where you are today. And by extension, understand that your current actions are leading you to where you'll be in the future.

What you decide to do today and every other day moving forward really matters! If you're not happy with your "today" life, then you must change your actions and decisions to create a better "future" life.

You start that process with an audit. One of the easiest ways to audit yourself is by asking four questions:

What are the things in my life that are not working that I should **stop** doing?

What are the things that I'm currently not doing that I need to **start** doing?

What are the things in my life that I should **change** to improve my life?

What are the things in my life that are really working that I should **continue** doing?

STOP	CONTINUE
START	CHANGE

WHAT ARE THE THINGS IN MY LIFE
THAT ARE NOT WORKING THAT
I SHOULD STOP DOING?

1 _____

2 _____

3 _____

4 _____

5 _____

WHAT ARE THE THINGS THAT I'M NOT
CURRENTLY DOING THAT I NEED
TO START DOING?

1 _____

2 _____

3 _____

4 _____

5 _____

WHAT ARE THE THINGS IN MY LIFE
THAT ARE REALLY WORKING THAT
I SHOULD CONTINUE DOING?

1
2
3
4
5

WHAT ARE THE THINGS IN MY LIFE
THAT I SHOULD CHANGE TO
IMPROVE MY LIFE?

1
2
3
4
5

To commit to your audit more fully, take some time to write down your answers. You'll refer to them often over the coming weeks and months. Answer honestly, even if you don't like what you're about to write.

If you cheat and soft-pedal this part of your audit, you're simply wasting your time. You're still too full of bullshit and not full of enough commitment to succeed in what you're about to do.

SERVE IT OVER THE NET

Imagine watching the Wimbledon finals, and your favorite tennis player is serving. The first serve slams into the net. *Fault.* They hit their second serve into the net, too. *Double fault.* You think, "Damn, that was stupid!"

They serve again and hit another ball into the net, exact same spot. And again, they hit their second serve into the net for another double fault. Now you're pissed. "What the hell are they doing?"

Unfortunately, a lot of us double-fault our way through life. We make the same mistakes over and over, and don't give ourselves a chance to win. In tennis, unforced errors lead to points for an opponent. In life, unforced errors lead to problems you could have and should have avoided.

Cheating on your partner is an unforced error that

leads to relationship problems. Repeatedly blowing up at your colleagues creates significant morale and retention problems. Running up credit card debt is an unforced error that can create financial, relationship, and trust issues with long-lasting repercussions.

What are the unforced errors in your life? What are you doing consciously and unconsciously to undermine your own efforts? Answering these questions, along with the four questions above, helps you start understanding where you're at and where you want to go.

WHAT ARE THE UNFORCED ERRORS IN YOUR LIFE?

1 _____

2 _____

3 _____

4 _____

5 _____

DEFINING SUCCESS

One day, I stepped out of an NBA All-Star's $300,000 Ferrari and as we were walking into his $25 million penthouse, he turned to me and said, "Man, life isn't fair."

His life wasn't fair? In a super-sarcastic tone, I said, "Yeah, your life really sucks. You're an NBA All-Star that has a couple of mansions, an unreal car collection, you've made a hundred million dollars, and you spend your weekends hooking up with supermodels."

Without pausing, he responded, "Man, I'd give all that shit away to feel amazing."

Here I was, a twenty-one-year-old college basketball player and entrepreneur who skipped party after party because I was hell-bent on becoming successful, and this player just dropped an incredible insight into what real success is all about.

I'd give all this shit away to feel amazing.

That's when it hit me. Success isn't about making a huge amount of money, getting a fancy job with a title you can brag about, or having a perfect body that you can post all over social media. Success is about feeling good, having internal peace, and being proud of the life you're living. I know for a fact there are plenty of billionaires and celebrities that would trade all their external success for internal peace.

As part of your audit, ask yourself if you're adopting someone else's definition of success or truly creating your own.

The great thing about life is that you get to decide what "winning" and "success" look like, as well as what "losing" and "failure" look like, and you can change these definitions whenever you desire.

THE INVISIBLE YOU

Everybody's wants are different. Our journeys are unique. But at the end of the day, we're all just trying to get to a place where we find happiness and inner peace. We want to be true to ourselves and proud of who we really are. If you're continuously rationalizing why you're not living your *best* life, you're way overdue for an audit of your *current* life.

We feel like shit when we know we're full of shit—when our feelings on the inside don't match how the world sees us and how we see ourselves on the outside. Living with your bullshit is a draining experience. Being inauthentic and putting on a show all day long robs you of so many things. Yet that's exactly what most people do. It's a form of insanity to live this way.

Many of us think we're emotionally tough and that we can simply push our past to the side. Just like earthquakes', our faults often remain hidden under the surface and are the result of things that happened a long time ago. And those faults can rupture at any time.

When we try pushing our past to the side, we end up pushing it even deeper inside us, which makes our problems even more challenging. The invisible you is even more important than the visible you. And no matter how hard you try to run away from your problems, you can't outrun what's inside you.

> *NO MATTER HOW HARD YOU TRY TO RUN AWAY FROM YOUR PROBLEMS, YOU CAN'T OUTRUN WHAT'S INSIDE YOU.*

It's like a big game of hide-and-seek, only with much higher stakes. We're not physically hiding behind the couch or under blankets like we did as kids. Instead, we're hiding some of our darkest truths and biggest secrets, hoping that others never find out about them. What makes this game even more twisted is that we go to such lengths to keep our deepest truths hidden, not just from others but also from ourselves. It's like we're silently praying that if we bury those dark secrets deep enough, they might just disappear for good.

Instead of hiding, ask yourself:

WHAT PARTS OF YOUR LIFE MAKE YOU FEEL LIKE A FRAUD?

1 _____

2 _____

3 _____

4 _____

5 _____

WHAT DO YOU NOT LIKE ABOUT YOUR LIFE THAT YOU HOPE NO ONE ELSE KNOWS ABOUT IT?

1 _____

2 _____

3 _____

4 _____

5 _____

WHAT ARE YOU AFRAID OF THAT
SOMEONE MIGHT CALL YOU OUT ABOUT?

1 _____

2 _____

3 _____

4 _____

5 _____

WHAT IS THE WORST-CASE SCENARIO
IF YOUR DARKEST SECRET WAS REVEALED
TO THE WORLD?

_____

_____

_____

_____

_____

What parts of your life make you feel like a fraud?

What do you not like about your life that you hope no one else knows about it?

What are you afraid of that someone might call you out about?

What is the worst-case scenario if your darkest secret was revealed to the world?

The answers to these questions are guiding your life more than you know.

No matter how good people's filtered lives look on social media, everyone has things they want to change in their world.

There is a reason most people have hundreds of Instagram posts, but thousands of pictures and videos on their camera. Social media is the "greatest hits" part of their lives. They only want followers to see their bests, not their norms.

People want you to see them holding hands with their loved one. They don't want you to see them bickering and arguing when the camera is off. They want you to see them traveling around the world. But they don't want you to know they flew on a discount airline and had three layovers.

Some of the coolest things you see on social media are posted by people who cry themselves to sleep at night, feel empty when they're by themselves, and wish their lives were half as amazing in real life as they're portrayed on Instagram.

We see their blessings and not their burdens. Social media feeds the fantasy. The invisible you that nobody sees is your stark reality check. Never forget that.

When you conduct your audit, zero in on the invisible parts of your life. It's in these often overlooked areas that you might uncover the real keys to understanding and improving yourself.

HIDDEN TRUTHS AND JUSTIFIABLE EXCUSES

Happiness doesn't come from lying to yourself and others about what's going on in your life. It comes from maintaining perspective during challenging times while finding solutions to resolve the problems that you're facing so you can get back to better times.

REGARDLESS OF HOW WELL YOU PORTRAY YOUR LIFE TO OTHERS, YOU CAN'T FOOL YOURSELF.

Regardless of how well you portray your life to others, you can't fool yourself. While it's easy to fake hustle, inspiration, and motivation to others, it's impossible to keep operating at a high level when you know you're faking it.

You also can't use others to justify your excuses.

Your partner's decision to skip the gym shouldn't be an excuse for you to do the same! You can't use their bad habits as a justification for your own laziness. Also, you can't play the "How do I stack up?" game. Just because you may not be as overweight as your best friend doesn't mean it's acceptable for you to carry a few extra pounds.

Comparison is a deadly form of bullshit.

Trying to make yourself feel better by claiming that you eat better or exercise more than your least healthy friend only means both of you have rude awakenings when health issues catch up down the road. Bragging about outworking your laziest teammate might seem like a flex, but in reality, it just means neither of you is on the path to superstardom. And photoshopping your Instagram pictures so that you look hotter than your friends doesn't make you prettier in real life.

I hate lies. I hate excuses. And so should you. Don't tolerate them from others.

More important, don't tolerate them from yourself.

SETTLING SUCKS

If you really dig deep into that honest place within yourself, chances are you'll be stunned and disturbed by how many poor choices you're responsible for in your life.

It could be a crappy marriage, a dead-end career, legal troubles, health issues, overbearing relatives, a shitty boss, and the list goes on. By now, you know who's to blame for all of this.

It's you.

You've settled. Somewhere along the way, you decided it was easier to give in than to fight. You've convinced yourself to tolerate less-than-ideal aspects of your life, and that's precisely what you've done. You bullshitted yourself into a tough spot, and now you either don't care or don't know what to do about it.

People live extraordinary lives because they haven't settled. Others struggle because they've created reasons, excuses, and justifications that give them an out.

Finding excuses is easy. Ignoring them is hard.

One day in the summer of 2012, I got a call from a mom named Brandy Cole asking me to train her son.

I have parents ask me to train their kids all the time, but this conversation was memorable because after I politely declined, she said, "I'll take out a loan to pay you if I have to." Brandy wanted the best for her son and wasn't going to settle for no as an answer.

I told her it wasn't about the money; I just preferred to focus on a few individuals instead of spreading myself thin by taking on everyone.

Still determined to make it happen, Brandy reached out to Brad Beal, who was one of the few high school players I was working with and asked for his help. Brandy had played high school volleyball under Brad's mom, Besta Beal, so the families were close.

Later that day, Brad called me and said, "Lil J is like a brother to me. Can you do me a favor and help him out?"

Because of how close I was to Brad, I agreed to work Lil J out.

Back then, load management wasn't a thing, so *all* my workouts were grueling. But I always made sure my first workout with a player was extra intense. That way, I could see what they were made of.

During our first workout, I pushed Lil J so hard that he had to leave the gym twice to vomit. But he pushed through and finished the workout.

About fifteen minutes after he left me, I got a call from his mom. I thought she was going to be mad at me. Instead, she said, "My son thought he was going to pass out. But you'll love this. He said that you were going to have to carry him off that court, because he wasn't going to give up."

That's when I knew Jayson Tatum was special.

The next workout, he told me that he wanted to follow in Brad Beal's footsteps. Brad had just been named Gatorade National Player of the Year.

I explained to him all the work that Brad put in—early-morning skill workouts, daily lifts, and late-night shooting sessions—and that Jayson's next four years were going to be that brutal workout we just went through, but Every. Single. Day. Jayson nodded and said, "I'm with it."

I put together a long-term development plan for him. We started meeting at his high school at 6 A.M. every morning to work out before school.

I told him that even though he was just a freshman I was going to use the same methodology that I used with my pro clients, developing one skill at a time by mastering the nuances contained within it.

Jayson idolized Kobe Bryant, so it was only right that we started with the mid-post, specifically the jab step. We watched film of Kobe, Michael Jordan, Carmelo Anthony, Tracy McGrady, and Kevin Durant, some of the wings who I wanted to model his game after. Then we walked through, talked through, and worked on every detail of a few different types of jabs.

As Jayson recalls, we went most of the first week without shooting a single jump shot.

Most kids his age wouldn't have had the patience to spend that much time on footwork, but Jayson wanted to be great. He understood that improvement takes time and embraced the struggle that comes with learning something new.

Jayson continued to master different aspects of his game, one skill at a time, throughout his high school career, something he continues to do to this day.

Like Brad, Jayson was named Gatorade National Player of the Year. Like Brad, he was picked third in the NBA Draft. And like Brad, he became one of the top stars in the league.

Weird coincidence? Nope. Just two guys who never settled.

SMASHING YOUR BULLSHIT HABITS

You work hard throughout the week, pulling in a decent income from your chosen profession, so it's only natural to give yourself a pat on the back for taking care of business when the weekend arrives. But what's not acceptable is when this self-congratulatory thinking becomes a rationale for continuously postponing that important project you've been saying you're going to get to for one more weekend. You're bullshitting yourself by thinking you've earned the right to keep pushing it off.

When the sun is shining, it's tempting to convince yourself that it's too beautiful to resist taking your dog for a long walk, going on a hike, or meeting up with friends at a park or the beach. On rainy days, you might easily sell yourself on the idea that there's nothing better than taking a nap during a downpour, curling up with a good book on the couch, or binge-watching Netflix for the next six hours. It's so easy to fall into these bullshit excuses, just like you've done countless times before.

Excuses are the shiny objects that distract you from doing the important work that will make a big difference in your life in the long run. It's often tempting to justify indulging in activities that offer immediate pleasure rather than tackling your biggest challenges.

That project goes from "I'll get it done this weekend" to "*Maybe* I'll get it done at some point in the future" to "Well, life went by fast, too bad I never got around to it." All because you opted for instant gratification, instead of investing the necessary time and effort to get the project done.

Think of how many bullshit habits there are in your life right now. Maybe you catch yourself snacking endlessly whenever boredom or anxiety starts to creep in. It could be that you consistently find yourself stressing for running late to appointments. Or you might notice a tendency to become confrontational and start fights for no good reason after consuming a few drinks.

The Audit forces you to study what your bullshit habits are and then figure out why you feel the way you do when specific things trigger you. The more you understand these connections, the more you can control and eliminate them.

YOU ARE A SELF-DECEPTION EXPERT

You are a self-deception expert. We are all self-deception experts. None of us can come close to counting how many lies we tell ourselves. We fool ourselves into believing things that are false and refuse to believe things that are true. Our lies range from small falsehoods that appear harmless to huge, life-altering whoppers that shape the way we see the world.

A lie protects your self-esteem. When you don't get a response after texting a crush, you may think that they simply didn't see the message instead of accepting the fact that they weren't interested. Other times, you lie to justify your shortcomings. You don't get college scholarship offers and blame it on any number of excuses instead of admitting that you simply weren't good enough or didn't work hard enough.

Most of the time, deep down, you know you're lying to yourself, but the tricky part is when you don't. Sometimes you start to believe your lies so deeply that they no longer appear to be untrue.

The irony is that we lie to avoid pain, but when we do, it hurts our chances of finding happiness in the long run.

PAY ATTENTION TO YOUR "CHECK ENGINE" LIGHTS

My dad handed me the keys to a car on my sixteenth birthday. Far from fancy, it was a 1992 Toyota Corolla with 194,000 miles on it and a big-ass dent in the driver-side door. My dad bought it for $300 and a box of steaks from his butcher shop. Seriously.

I didn't care about the dent, the miles, the year, the make, or the model. I had a car!

To put my personal touch on it, I installed two twelve-inch subs and added an incredible sound system that cost double what my dad paid for the car. I'm pretty sure a few of my neighbors got to know the lyrics to "Go DJ" by Lil Wayne because of how loud I bumped my music driving to and from the gym and school every day.

On the way to practice one day, my car broke down, and I ended up stranded on the side of a busy highway. The engine was shot, and it was my own fault. You see, that stupid little "check engine" light had been blinking for a while and I'd just been ignoring it.

The timing sucked. I had just started training players and only had a couple of thousand dollars in my bank account. I couldn't afford the car I wanted, but I found a used 1998 Nissan Pathfinder for sale for $2,400 that would get me back on the road.

Appearance-wise, it was an upgrade, but the car wouldn't start if it rained, snowed, or was too cold. That's a pretty big problem during a Midwest winter. When I took it to the mechanic, they said it would cost $800 to fix it. There was no way I was going to spend a third of what I paid for the car on a small problem that I could solve by simply getting someone to jump-start me.

Instead, I decided to get all the windows tinted and add twenty-inch rims for around the same price. That *small* issue that would have cost me $800 to fix ended up costing me way more in the long run.

First, I bought a portable jump starter to throw into the back of my car when I needed it. Then I bought a new battery and alternator. Because I hired cheap help to install those things, the wiring got messed up, and I was forced to buy a new starter. It was one thing after the next.

Back-to-back cars, I made the same mistake. I didn't take care of the issues under the hood.

Talk about a life lesson . . .

I'm sure you can list several times when you didn't pay attention to your "check engine" lights and the painful lessons you had to learn as a result. I can tell you now, when a "check engine" light comes on in my life, I check it ASAP!

Too often, we ignore the "check engine" lights in our lives. We don't take the time to handle the *small* problems that end up becoming *big* problems that cost us a lot more. It's time to stop ignoring your "check engine" lights. Check under your own hood with an audit of what's causing the problems in your life.

WHAT ARE THE SMALL PROBLEMS IN YOUR LIFE THAT COULD END UP BECOMING BIG PROBLEMS IF YOU KEEP IGNORING THEM?

1

2

3

4

5

WHAT DO YOU NEED TO AUDIT?

Conducting an audit is essentially taking a thoughtful look at the aspects you love about your life and pinpointing areas you'd like to change. Audits aren't strictly black-and-white; there's a whole spectrum of gray where you might excel in some things but see room for improvement in others.

You can be financially secure and still aspire to more income. You can be a great parent or spouse in some ways while still wanting to do better in others.

The same applies to you. Loving who you are in this moment and desiring personal growth can absolutely coexist. In fact, they should complement each other. Keep excelling in the areas of your life where you're thriving, while simultaneously improving in the areas you're not.

To properly audit where you are, you must be super honest with yourself. And not just on a superficial level. This is not the time to say, "I'm fine," if there are areas of your life that you have been really wanting to improve. It's also not the time to settle for less than your best. Unrealized potential becomes pain, and you've lived with that pain far too long.

> UNREALIZED POTENTIAL BECOMES PAIN, AND YOU'VE LIVED WITH THAT PAIN FAR TOO LONG.

Surviving isn't enough. It's time to stop bullshitting yourself so you can start thriving! To thrive, you must get to the bottom of what's holding you back and dragging you down. And you must be as specific as possible.

Is it your family? Are there relatives who drain your energy, talk about you behind your back, or are jealous when you succeed? Who are they? Be specific!

Do you struggle with your weight? Are health issues making it difficult to keep off the unwanted pounds? Do you use food as an emotional crutch? Are other parts of your life depressing you to the point you don't care how you look and feel?

How is your financial situation? Struggling with sticking to your budget? Finding yourself attempting to spend your way out of the blues? Stuck in a job that doesn't pay well? Have you made investments that didn't quite work out over time? What factors contribute to your dysfunctional relationship with money?

What about your job? Dealing with a shitty boss? Finding your work routine dull and repetitive? Nervous about exploring opportunities with a new employer? Have you gone the extra mile to stand out and shine in your current position? How much does what you do for work define who you are as a person? And, when it comes to work-life balance, is it working for you, or do you feel there's room for improvement?

How is your emotional well-being? Are high levels of anxiety a challenge for you? Do you experience bouts of anger or depression? Is there a sense of worthlessness or a lack of self-confidence? Do you turn to drugs and alcohol as a way to cope with perceived pain? The alarming surge in substance abuse globally tells me there are a lot of unhappy people out there who would rather self-medicate than self-heal.

Everybody who audits themselves will come up with different answers. Each of us is a complex web of all the things I mentioned above, and so much more.

If you're still struggling to put your finger on why you aren't thriving, ask yourself how your best friend would answer that question for you. They know you the best. They're also who you usually vent to, and many times they're more brutally honest with you than you are with yourself.

Still can't figure it out? How about this thought exercise: Suppose I gave you a magic pill to cure anything that you are struggling with in your life. What would you use it on? Pick one thing and one thing only.

WHAT WOULD YOUR MAGIC PILL CURE?

_____

_____

_____

_____

_____

If you want to stop bullshitting yourself, you're not allowed to take a pass on the ways to audit who you are.

What is it that you need to audit? Keep digging until you get that answer. You may already know, or it could take days, weeks, months, or years of soul-searching to zero in on those parts of your life you need to improve, but don't stop until you do, because it will be worth it.

If it causes you a lot of discomfort to admit certain things, that's a healthy sign that you're doing the hard work of being honest with yourself.

As you go through this process, you'll compile a list that might have three things or might have twenty. There's no magic number. When in doubt, include everything that comes to mind, as you might be surprised by how one aspect can significantly impact others.

We tend to bullshit ourselves into believing we're great at compartmentalizing things, but in reality, we really suck at it. I see it all the time with athletes. Most of their slumps on the court start with stresses or struggles off the court.

An unfortunate and well-known instance of this occurred with my favorite golfer, Tiger Woods.

Tiger was the most dominant golfer ever during his prime. From 1996 onward, he has won 82 tournaments, including 15 major championships. Equally impressive is his remarkable consistency, winning at least one tournament each year from the period 1996 to 2009.

However, the trajectory of his career took an unexpected turn just after midnight on Thanksgiving in 2009 when his wife requested a divorce. Consequently, Tiger did not win another tournament until March 2012—almost two and a half years later.

Tiger openly admitted that the personal challenges he faced off the course impacted his performance on the course, acknowledging that they occasionally became so overwhelming that it was difficult to concentrate on shots at times.

Over the fourteen years since that pivotal night, Tiger has managed to win just one major championship—far from the unprecedented dominance he once exhibited.

Allowing challenges in one aspect of life to impact others is not exclusive to athletes.

Working parents know how easy it is for challenges in one area to spill over into the next. After a demanding day at work, when Mom or Dad finally steps through the front door, they try to throw on a happy face. They can keep up this act for a bit, but even the tiniest trigger—a child chewing loudly with their mouth wide open at the dinner table—can lead them to snap and lose their temper. Following an outburst of frustration, they abruptly get up and leave the table, ruining dinner for everyone. The noisy chewing was the "one more thing" to cap off a crappy day at a lousy job, and it needlessly dragged down another part of their life.

That's how our stresses and struggles work. Like fighting against a good boxer, they wear us down. Parts of our life jab us here and there, hit us in the ribs over and over, or land a haymaker on our chin, and before you know it, we can't take any more. We hit the canvas and we're down for the ten count.

The good news is many of these blows are avoidable if you know how to block them or outbox your opponents.

SCOUTING YOURSELF

Elite athletes and coaches spend countless hours breaking down film, trying to find opponents' weaknesses. They look for these weaknesses so they can build a game plan to take advantage of them. And when the stakes are the highest, in the playoffs, these scouting reports and game plans become even more vital to winning. That's why most teams print out binders that break down an opponent's offensive and defensive schemes and rotations, and detailed reports on player personnel that includes strengths, weaknesses, and other tendencies.

The challenges you face in life are not so different. You must scout yourself and identify your weaknesses so they don't take advantage of you. Understanding what could hold you back and where you could go wrong gives you the power to adjust and prevent errors before they occur.

Oftentimes, when people start making changes in their lives, they fail to spot their weak links. For instance, if you want to improve your financial well-being, you might concentrate solely on increasing income while overlooking poor spending habits—a critical weak link that contributes to your financial challenges.

Do you genuinely need every streaming service, or could canceling a few subscriptions ease financial strain? Is there room to cut back on nonessential expenses, like opting for a monthly rather than a weekly nail salon visit? And what if swapping nightly food delivery for cooking at home could alleviate some financial stress?

While those indulgences are nice, nothing compares to the feeling of financial security.

Another part of scouting yourself is avoiding the people, places, and things that tempt you to fall back into your bad habits. If you know you can't stop from checking who your ex is following, block them. When you know you'll be sucked into toxic conversations by certain people in your life, avoid them. If you know you'll cheat on your diet if you go out to eat, stay in.

Relying on self-control and willpower is a short-term strategy that rarely results in long-term success. It's like going into a fight expecting to knock out your opponent in the first round. That could happen, but if you haven't prepared for what might happen if things don't go as planned, you're going to be in trouble! Like Mike Tyson said, "Everyone has a plan until they get punched in the mouth."

You may be able to avoid drinking one night out, you may be able to pass the bread at the table without sneaking a piece, and you may be able to say "no, thank you" to dessert, but if you avoid that tempting dinner altogether, your probability of staying locked into your weight loss plan goes way up.

Optimizing your environment means making the right choices ahead of time, so you don't have to rely on pure willpower in the moment. Willpower is a finite resource, but no matter how hard you try, you have limits, and you will reach a point when you can't muster up more of it. The more structure you have and the more triggers you avoid, the less discipline you need.

WHAT ARE YOUR WEAK LINKS?

1.
2.
3.
4.
5. .

GAME PLAN TO OVERCOME THEM:

1.
2.
3.
4.
5.

WHAT ARE THE TRIGGERS (PEOPLE,
PLACES, AND THINGS) THAT TEMPT YOU
TO FALL BACK INTO YOUR BAD HABITS?

1 _____

2 _____

3 _____

4 _____

5 _____

STRATEGY TO DEFEAT THE TRIGGER:

1 _____

2 _____

3 _____

4 _____

5 _____

Your triggers and temptations have a weird way of showing up when you are most vulnerable. If you're not equipped with a plan when they present themselves, you probably won't like the outcome.

MAKE SURE LITTLE THINGS STAY LITTLE

Life doesn't suck no matter how bad things may seem. There may be an area or two of your life that is dragging you down, like a stressful job, an unhealthy relationship, or debt that you can't seem to escape. But you still have many things to be thankful for.

However, your entire life can feel like it sucks if you don't address the little things dragging you down. Little things are rarely little. They can have big impacts on our lives if we let them.

I see couples let little disagreements ruin their entire relationship. Does it matter if you get Mexican food or Italian food? Or whose turn it is to do the dishes? What if they forget to put the toilet seat down or don't ever put their shoes away?

If you're saying "yes, it matters," let me reframe the question: "Is it worth tearing your relationship apart?" Hopefully not! The question may be a bit of a dramatic example, but the point is that you need to put things in context. Understand what's worth elevating to a larger issue and what's worth letting go.

The next time an argument over something that's not important is brewing, ask yourself, "Would I rather be right or happy?" Odds are, winning that argument won't improve your life, but maintaining peace will. Don't waste your valuable time getting upset, stressed, or rattled over things that aren't a big deal. Keep the peace, and your peace, and move on.

WOULD I RATHER BE RIGHT OR HAPPY?

If you need to stand up for something you believe in, that's a different story. Even then, you should ask, "Is this fight worth losing my peace over?" Choose your battles wisely.

To assess the impact and importance of a certain situation, use The Rule of Three. Reflect on whether the current circumstances will hold significance three hours, three days, three months, or three years from now.

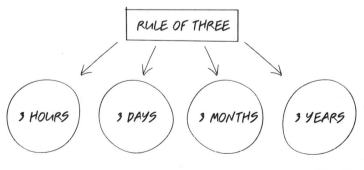

RULE OF THREE

3 HOURS 3 DAYS 3 MONTHS 3 YEARS

When you answer that question honestly, it creates a perspective on how irrelevant most things are when balanced against protecting your peace.

I'm guessing that if your child accidentally spills something in your car today, you won't be stressing out about it three years from now. Accidents happen. Keep your cool, clean up the mess, and move on.

Are you still going to be angry three months from now if someone messes up tonight's DoorDash dinner order? Call DoorDash. Figure out a way to fix the order, and don't let it ruin the movie night that you've been planning all week.

And is not getting enough "like"s on your latest post going to still bother you three days from now? Your grandparents dealt with the Great Depression and world wars. I hope you're not going to let Instagram's algorithm get you down.

Think back to all the small things you stressed about in the past. Imagine all the things you've wasted time stressing about that no longer matter.

Remember that test you failed in sixth grade that brought you to tears? Or that last-second play you messed up in the big rivalry game in high school that made you almost quit your favorite sport? What about that time some guy tailgated you on the highway for a couple of miles a few years ago? When is the last time anything like that stressed you out or impacted your life?

Keep small moments as small as they need to be. Making them bigger in your head for longer than you should is just a way to carry around mental baggage that gets heavier and heavier. Live by the philosophy that if it won't have a big impact in the future, don't let it have a big impact in the present.

It's hard to bring that kind of perspective to events when you're in the heat of the moment. But when you can let go of the little things that don't matter as quickly as possible, you free yourself up to focus on the big things that do matter. And the more you practice letting go of the little things, the easier it becomes over time.

YOUR RELATIONSHIP WITH RELATIONSHIPS

You also need to audit the people in your life. If people aren't helping you grow, you need to let them go. When someone is stressing you more than they are blessing you, they have to go. To become the best version of yourself, you can't let other people's bullshit weigh you down or hold you back. Trust me, you've got plenty of your own shit to deal with.

Part of improving your life is improving the quality

of people in your life. According to studies, your stress levels can rise after spending just two minutes around a negative person. If two minutes creates that strong of a reaction, imagine spending a lifetime in that environment. Like a yawn, the people around you are contagious.

As you change, your relationships with others will change too. Some will strengthen. Some will lessen. And some will die off completely.

Some of the people you associate with will be threatened as you make a move toward a better life. They may throw shade at you or question you for wanting to make changes, but that is jealousy or fear coming into play as they try to hold you back. They know that if you change and they don't, you might outgrow them, so they try to sabotage your growth to keep you in their lives.

You see this all the time. Ladies, have your friends ever shamed you for wanting to give up clubbing and alcohol? Staying in and sobering up could really improve your life, but they know the only time you hang out is when you're partying together, so if you give that up, you may give them up as well.

And for the men, has a wingman given you a hard time for jumping into a relationship? Being faithful to someone you really like could bring you a ton of happiness. But when your buddies know the main reason you hang out is to chase girls together, and you're ready to give that up, you may not spend as much time with them anymore.

They're putting their wants over your needs. But because you're done bullshitting yourself, you're no longer going to let that happen. You are going to finally choose what's best for you.

Auditing your relationships is one of the hardest parts of this process. You're going to be accused of being selfish when you cut people out of your life. This may seem like a hard thing to do, but if you're serious about improving your life, you'll find a way.

When you audit your relationships, you're also going to see who the real cheerleaders are in your life. Those people who support you even if it means adjusting the dynamics of your relationship are people you're likely to either keep in your life or reconnect with in the future. They're the kind of people you'll want in your life as you evolve into the new version of yourself.

EMBRACING YOUR SCARS

It's important to make peace with your past so it doesn't mess with you now and in the future.

If you had a great childhood full of wonderful experiences, you probably view the world positively and don't need to go back and audit much, unless you want to go back simply to relive the good memories.

Those of you who had a rough childhood or experienced trauma in your past probably view the world in a darker way and don't realize how much those monstrous, complicated, unpleasant memories are messing you up. That past will continue to keep an ugly grip on you if you let it.

Auditing your past can reveal the critical information you need to move beyond the bullshit that's been holding you back. Take a moment to consider how the past may have affected you, but avoid dwelling on it for too long. You don't want to get caught up in the mess of the past and unintentionally complicate things for yourself as you move forward.

I can't tell you how much time to audit your past is appropriate, but I can tell you that ignoring past trauma or attempting to bury it will only make matters worse. In fact, the feelings you suppress the most are often the ones that have the most significant impact on you.

If you tell yourself you aren't ready to dig into the past because you're not ready to deal with the pain that's associated with it, understand that not dealing with it forces you to keep dealing with it. The journey through your pain is a lot easier than the burden of holding on to that same pain.

Taking ownership of the bullshit from your past, regardless of whether it was your fault or not, takes you off the bench of victimhood, puts you on the court and into the game. And the court is the only place you can impact the games that are taking place in your head and heart . . . the ones you have to win to reclaim your inner peace.

THE JOURNEY THROUGH YOUR PAIN IS A LOT EASIER THAN THE BURDEN OF HOLDING ON TO THAT SAME PAIN.

What I'm about to tell you next is extremely important.

If you've experienced some really bad shit and you don't think you can deal with it on your own, *get professional help.* Not getting help when you genuinely need it is also a form of bullshitting yourself. In fact, it's one of the riskiest, highest-stakes games of bullshit you can play. And sometimes, the outcomes are not good unless you recognize your limits and get the support you need for dealing with stuff you can't handle on your own.

SEE YOUR SCARS

I have scars. You have scars. Everybody has scars. Anybody who tells you they don't probably has the biggest and nastiest scars of all.

I'm not talking about the scars you get from falling on the playground, crashing your bike, or roughhousing with your brothers and sisters as a kid. I'm talking about the emotional scars that come from painful moments in our childhoods.

Maybe other kids laughed at you because you couldn't pronounce a word correctly when asked to read in front of the class, and you developed a fear that you weren't very smart. Perhaps your grandma called you chunky, and you began to think that you weren't attractive or had to keep a perfect physique and that criticism has stuck with you. Or you watched your parents argue throughout your childhood and now fear committing to a relationship.

The longer we hold on to these beliefs, the deeper we connect to them, and the less aware we are that they color how we see ourselves and our world now.

> THE LONGER WE HOLD ON TO BELIEFS, THE DEEPER WE CONNECT TO THEM.

These scars impact our inner selves, and they manifest outwardly in behaviors that often work against us. To overcome our pasts, we try to hide our scars or overcompensate for them. Neither action is healthy.

It's not your fault that shitty things happened in your childhood; don't blame yourself if you tend to generalize about yourself and the world based on your past experiences. But it is your fault if you continue to let those experiences hold you back.

Most of the time the deepest scars form early in life. You were so young and didn't know what these things meant and didn't realize that you would one day have the power to put meaning behind things that happened to you years ago. Time has a way of creating a perspective that allows you to put in context what these moments mean. Once you understand this, you can eliminate the negative narratives that have hurt you, once and for all.

Most of the time, people find ways to go forward. But underneath, the scars become a part of them and impact *how* they go forward.

For example, as an adult, you consider yourself a perfectionist. You're not sure why. You just *know* that being a perfectionist suits you. You may not remember that this could have stemmed from an innocent comment your grandma made when she saw your mom give you some candy as a kid: "No wonder she's got a belly. All you do is keep giving her sweets."

Your grandma directed those words at your mom and was trying to look out for your health and emotional wellness, because she struggled with weight and insecurity issues throughout her life, but you took them to heart, and they stung deeply because you loved your grandma and craved her love and approval.

While that one offhand comment may have melted away from your consciousness, deep down, it stayed with you and never fully went away. And it produced an ugly scar.

Now, imagine taking that one moment and multiplying it by hundreds of similar experiences. Whether they were misguided, misunderstood, or careless comments or actions at the time, they all left a lasting impression on you. Can you see why you probably carry countless scars as a result?

Other people can love you, make you happy, sympathize with, support, or encourage you, but what they can't do is heal you. You're the only person who can do that. What you don't fully heal from will affect you in some way. Your scars could start bleeding at any time, and chances are you'll end up bleeding on people who didn't hurt you. Inevitably, however, the person you end up bleeding on the most is yourself.

WHAT EMOTIONAL SCARS FROM YOUR PAST ARE STILL IMPACTING YOU TODAY?

1 _____

2 _____

3 _____

4 _____

5 _____

PLAN TO PERMANENTLY HEAL OR OVERCOME THE SCAR:

1 _____

2 _____

3 _____

4 _____

5 _____

THE GAP

When you conduct a comprehensive audit, you can start to spot the gaps between where you are and where you want to be.

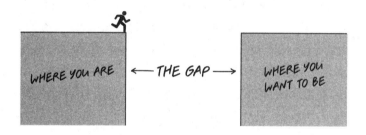

The Gap is a snapshot of where you are now and the beginning of the road map you're going to flesh out. It's critical because you can't get to where you want to be unless you know where you need to go.

You may be tempted to breeze over this step because you're anxious to get going based on what you've uncovered about yourself. That would be a mistake.

Pinpointing your gaps is a critical gut check when you want to stop bullshitting yourself.

Think of it this way. Let's say you're hiking to a secluded beach that you've always dreamed of visiting. An hour into your hike, you come to the banks of a large river. You know from your map that a bridge should be here, only to discover the bridge has been wiped out by recent heavy rains.

The little voice in your head tells you, "Shit! Now what? How do I get to where I want to be with a huge obstacle standing in my way?" You consider the possibility of giving up and turning back to where you parked your car, several miles away. "Going back is easier. It's also safer. There's no way to cross this damn river" is a little conversation you have with yourself while weighing what to do next.

Your gaps in life are exactly like trying to cross that river. If you really want to get to that secluded beach on the other side, you've got to find a way to overcome the difficult gaps standing in your way.

You need to consider your options while also assessing your level of desire.

"Is there a shallow crossing downstream? How far is the next bridge upstream? Is there a way to rig ropes so that I can safely get across? How bad do I want to get across?"

When you're facing The Gap, only you know for sure

what you're willing to do and how motivated you are to do it.

IDENTIFYING THE GAP

In the summer of 2019, Brad Beal walked into the gym and I asked him a straightforward question: "Do you think you can average thirty points per game?"

After a brief pause, Brad responded, "Thirty points, bro? Do you know how hard it is to average thirty points per game in the NBA?"

As a lifelong basketball fan, I was well aware of the rarity of averaging thirty points per game. In Brad's lifetime, only ten players had achieved this feat. And despite only one player topping thirty points per game the previous season, I still knew Brad was more than capable. He was one of the best players in the world and coming off back-to-back All-Star selections.

He had just averaged a career high of 25.6 points per game, so I thought the best strategy to get him to believe it was possible was to shift the focus from reaching the 30-point mark to narrowing the gap of 4.4 points.

Building off the previous season's success, all he had to do was attempt one more three-point shot, one more two-point shot, and draw one extra shooting foul per game to give him two more free throws.

After reframing the goal this way, Brad now had the confidence that he could do it.

In 2020, he averaged 30.5 points per game and an even-more impressive 31.3 points per game in the 2021 season.

Now, I want you to determine The Gap you need to shrink the most.

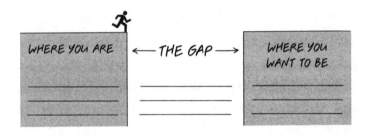

After you identify The Gap, I want you to reframe it just like Brad.

For instance, if you dream of owning a new car, and it requires a $10,000 down payment, but you only have $2,700 in your bank account, The Gap is $7,300. Initially, it might seem like a lot of money, but when you break it down, it's only $20 per day for a year. To put it into perspective, my little nieces and nephews make more than that running a lemonade stand for an hour!

Or let's say you want to lose fifty pounds. It might feel unrealistic, but if you shift your perspective to losing one pound a week, your goal suddenly sounds way more manageable.

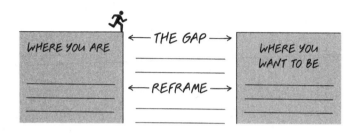

Identifying The Gap between where you are and where you want to be is important; however, an even more crucial step is reframing The Gap into a series of smaller changes, such as setting a feasible daily savings target or shedding a few ounces each day, so that your goal becomes more realistic and achievable.

THE ACTION GAP

If you're like many people, you say all the right things, but don't do all the right things. These can be the conversations with little voices inside your head, or those, out loud, with people in your life. You claim you're willing to do anything and everything to turn your life around *until* it's time to do anything and everything to turn your life around.

I call this the Action Gap.

It's easy to talk shit but much harder to back it up.

> IT'S EASY TO TALK SHIT
> BUT MUCH HARDER TO BACK IT UP.

You say you want six-pack abs, to spend more time with your family, or to end a toxic relationship. But when it's time to walk the walk, you're not willing to diet and workout, spend less time at work, or cut ties with someone who isn't right for you.

You can talk about how you want to change something in your life until you're blue in the face. But if you aren't willing to do the work to get what you say you want, the truth is that you don't want it as bad as you claim you do. That's The Gap. Your actions, not your desires, reveal what you really want.

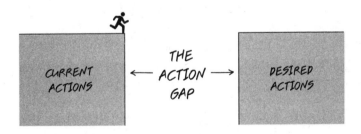

If you really wanted more free time, you'd start respecting your time more by saying no to unnecessary meetings, meet-ups, or events. Suppose you genuinely want to achieve greater financial security; you might consider taking on an additional job to earn extra income and cut down on unnecessary spending. Let's say you want to stop stressing out so much. First you audit, then avoid the people, situations, and places that create that stress.

When you really want to make changes in your life, you need to be willing to do the things that those changes require! What you intend to do amounts to absolutely zero if you don't actually do it.

Good intentions with shitty execution produces shitty results. What's even more detrimental is when you fail to address that gap, leading to feelings of anger, frustration, and lashing out, ultimately pushing your goals farther from where you want to be.

To prevent you from becoming a victim of the Action Gap, refer to The Gap you just identified. List the current actions that are keeping you where you are and the actions that will propel you to where you want to be.

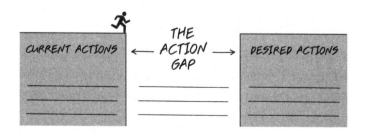

Focusing on your gaps forces you to envision your life in a year, ten years, or twenty-five years down the road. Start thinking about what you want, how to get those things, and what you'll need to add and subtract in your life to get you there. After all, it's hard to get somewhere if you don't know where you want to go.

The gap also compels you to ask an even more fundamental and essential question: What do you REALLY want in life?

Answering that question isn't easy for many people. At one time or another, you might have envied people who knew they were destined to be doctors, pilots, teachers, or military service members since they were young. That doesn't mean they have an easier journey than you. It simply means they've been more focused from the get-go, with more time to close The Gap between where they are and where they want to be. If they've made the right choice, they're also filled with passion, making it easier to overcome the obstacles we all face.

If you don't have a clear answer yet, spend some time thinking about what you want. Have those honest conversations with yourself. But don't fall into the trap of "someday" thinking. Once you do figure it out and you're filled with excitement and passion of your own, take your life out of park and shove it into gear. Then hit the gas pedal.

SHRINK YOUR GAPS

Your gaps add a ton of stress, insecurity, and anxiety to your life.

Identifying your gaps; eliminating the bullshit thoughts, feelings, emotions, and excuses that have created those gaps; and then strategizing what steps you can take to shrink them is what frees you from those feelings.

For example, when you stress about your weight, you're really stressing about the gap that exists between the body you have and the body you want. The longer the gap exists, the more the gap weighs on you. Pun intended!

But The Gap isn't solely the twenty pounds you want to lose. There's also a gap between the actions that are keeping you twenty pounds overweight and the actions necessary to shed those pounds. It might be related to portion sizes or the types of food you're consuming. Late-night snacking out of boredom could be a factor. Or perhaps spending too much time around people with unhealthy eating habits is influencing your own choices.

You must figure out why The Gap you want to close remains in your life before you can come up with ways to shrink it.

Take some time to list why you've allowed The Gap to remain until now and why you're finally committed to closing The Gap.

WHY HAVE YOU ALLOWED
THE GAP TO REMAIN?

_____

_____

_____

_____

_____

_____

WHY ARE YOU FINALLY COMMITTED
TO CLOSING THE GAP?

_____

_____

_____

_____

_____

_____

Gaps are in opposition to you living your best life so treat them like the enemies they are. Stop tolerating and accepting them as parts of your life and start figuring out how to make critical changes to shrink or eliminate them.

Avoid blaming others or aspects of your life that you settle for if there's a gap that's solvable. This is on YOU, and you alone. The decision to shrink a gap or live with it is entirely yours. Self-accountability is paramount in this process.

Choosing between these two paths is a decisive action. If you're not willing to actively work toward shrinking the gaps you have, you are essentially choosing to let those gaps remain in your life.

Shrinking those gaps is hard. The fundamental question to ask yourself is, "Am I okay with being miserable by allowing my gaps to remain, or would I rather do what it takes to shrink them and make myself happy?" Seems like an easy choice to me.

YOU'RE NOT AT THE TOP YET, MISTER

During my junior year in high school, I took an official visit to the University of Pennsylvania after they offered me a basketball scholarship. I brought my high school coach, Jay Blossom, with me.

After meeting with the coaching staff, scrimmaging

with the players, and touring the school, we decided to explore Philadelphia.

One of our first stops was the Philadelphia Museum of Art, which features the famous steps Rocky ran up before his big fight with Apollo Creed. Coach Blossom was a social studies teacher and sports lover, so this was a massive highlight for him. At the bottom of the steps, he asked me to film his epic run to the top. When he got to the top, he started air boxing and celebrating, mimicking Rocky.

After about ten seconds of this, a kid no older than six years old walked by him and said, "Hey, mister, you're not even at the top yet." The kid pointed to another set of stairs that Coach Blossom did not even realize were there. My coach shook his head, started laughing, and told me to delete the footage before we walked down to the bottom to try again.

Often, we think we're at the top or doing our best when, in reality, there's another level we're unaware of that we need to climb to completely close The Gap. Sometimes, we figure that out when we're climbing those stairs. Other times, it takes someone else to point out the obvious to us.

Always assume there's another level. Climb those stairs to close The Gap, but never assume that just because you believe you've reached the top, you've truly made it to the summit.

Do a gut check. Then do another. The last thing you want to do is think you're at the top of the stairs when, in reality, you're not. That only sets you up for more frustration and potential failure in the future. Know there is always room for growth.

THE ART OF SELF-SABOTAGE

While I empathize with most people, I don't feel sorry for anyone who can make changes but refuses to do so.

Some people are so good at self-sabotage that they've made it an art form. Instead of channeling their energy, creativity, and intelligence to create something positive in their lives, they waste it creating colorful lies to deceive themselves.

This description may resonate with you because, at one point or another, we all become masters of self-deception.

Deep down, we love distractions, because they provide a convenient escape from facing challenges or truths that we're afraid of or simply want to avoid.

We also have a bad habit of downplaying our goals. We try to convince ourselves that we don't want that dream house or the perfect relationship because deep down, we're not sure we're worthy or if those goals are even attainable.

And then, when we start thinking about all the effort needed to reach our goals, doubt creeps in, so we end up creating these stories, telling ourselves it's all too hard, the odds are stacked against us, or the world's just too messed up to let us get what we want.

We blend these distractions, downplays, and doubts to create self-sabotaging masterpieces. The problem is that when we paint these masterpieces, we're really painting ourselves into a corner of life that's way below what we actually deserve.

The key to closing gaps is to pay attention to these behaviors and call yourself out every time you catch yourself falling into them.

It's not easy because, many times, you've been justifying and rationalizing your self-sabotaging bullshit behaviors since you were a kid. It takes practice to spot distractions, downplays, and doubts. The more you consciously pay attention to them, the easier it gets to kick them to the curb.

Crossing the rivers in your life is the only way to get to the other side. I know this sounds cliché and obvious, but you have to take the time to figure out what your gaps are, identify why you've allowed them to remain, and devise strategies to overcome them. Only then can you cross the river.

THE
DECISION

You can define what bullshit is, audit yourself, and identify all the gaps you should work on to eliminate your bullshit. But until you decide enough is enough and you're no longer going to allow that bullshit to remain in your life, you'll keep settling and feeling trapped, frustrated, anxious, depressed, and insecure.

You must dig deep and find powerful, compelling reasons to make changes, or finally get so fed up with the gaps you have allowed to remain in your life that you finally decide to take action to shrink them. Wanting to make changes does nothing. Deciding you are going to make changes does everything.

Every change starts with a moment. Every change requires a new mindset and needs to be backed with enough meaning to follow through.

THE MOMENT

Have many times have you said these things?

"One day, I will . . ." followed by something you could be doing now.

"I would, but . . ." followed by an excuse that you could easily overcome.

"I wish I could . . ." followed by a realistic goal if you just made a few pivots in your life.

People struggling with obesity make peace with their health issues by claiming food makes them happy and they're comfortable in their bodies. Those who struggle with finances justify being poor by saying money isn't everything. They convince themselves that they don't care if they're in shape or financially stable. But if you offered them a magic pill that would give them a slim and strong athletic body without having to exercise or eat healthy or offered them money with no strings attached, they'd gladly accept.

Some don't want to believe that they have the power to change the bullshit in their lives because that puts responsibility in their hands.

They'd rather blame their circumstances, the way they were raised, bad luck, genetics, or a thousand other excuses because that's easy. But it doesn't solve anything.

There are a ton of people who came from abusive, negligent families who are thriving either as successful businesspeople or as awesome parents. Others have worked two or three jobs to put themselves through school to become doctors, tech superstars, teachers, police officers, scientists, or other professionals who are making a positive impact.

I coach the most talented NBA players in the world, who often rose from modest beginnings to become incredibly wealthy and well-known. Many of them use their success as a platform for causes they believe in, such as Brad Beal, who won the NBA's Community Assist Award for his ongoing charity work. Or Jayson Tatum, who, through his foundation, inspires and positively impacts St. Louis children and teens by incorporating education, athletics, and mentorship into their lives.

Living a life marked by resilience and success doesn't just happen by chance. What these individuals have in common is they've all made an intentional decision to reject the shortcomings of their lives. They navigate through challenges with dedication, hard work, and an unwavering commitment to their dreams. Giving up is not an option as they consistently work toward creating a better, more fulfilling life for themselves and others.

Focusing on the benefits of changing instead of the difficulties of making the changes often helps you get to the moment where you finally act.

Every time you're put to a decision involving change, ask yourself, "Would I rather make difficult changes and fix my problem or live a difficult life and have that problem haunt me for as long as I avoid the changes?"

If you want to make changes to improve your life but you're still rationalizing your bullshit with "justifiable" excuses, take it a step further. You're only in a "desire" stage and not a "decision" stage. There is a big difference between the two. You can desire to improve your life until the end of time, but until you decide to improve your life, nothing will change. Desires are part of magical "if" thinking.

> "If my boyfriend would magically stop flirting with other people while we're out, then our relationship would be perfect!"

> "If my brother would magically stop drinking so much at birthdays, Thanksgiving, and Christmas, our family gatherings would be so much better!"

> "If my terrible boss would magically resign, this job wouldn't be so bad!"

Magical thinking, just like magic itself, is an illusion. Stop thinking that way and stop clinging to false hopes. If you want something to change, start taking matters into your own hands.

Talk to your boyfriend and tell him that overt flirting

is unacceptable and could lead to your breakup. If he keeps it up, he doesn't love or respect you and it's time to leave. Tell your brother that his drinking is ruining gatherings. Tell him to stop and if he doesn't, uninvite him in the future. Your boss isn't going anywhere, so either try repairing your relationship with them or explore new job opportunities that offer you a healthier and more satisfying work environment.

Taking matters into your own hands and communicating openly are more effective approaches to resolving issues than hoping for magical solutions. If you want your life to change, you must be the catalyst for that change.

The Decision is deeper than wanting to change. It's *needing* to change. It's the difference between saying the right things and doing the right things. That also means being mentally strong enough to adjust and stick with those changes long after your initial burst of motivation wears off.

Every great change starts with The Moment you decide that you will no longer tolerate what is holding you back.

To get to The Moment, you must stop beating around the bush, sugarcoating the lies you tell yourself, and sweeping things under the rug.

I mentioned it before, but it's worth repeating: be prepared to dig deep and have some uncomfortable and honest conversations with yourself. I can't tell you what those conversations are. You'll need to figure that out for yourself. I do know the conversations you've been putting off the longest and are most afraid to have are the ones you need the most.

> THE CONVERSATIONS YOU'VE BEEN PUTTING OFF THE LONGEST AND ARE THE MOST AFRAID TO HAVE ARE THE ONES YOU NEED THE MOST.

If you wait for *a* moment, it may never come, which is why you must create *The* Moment: by looking in the mirror and soul-searching, realizing you deserve better.

The Moment is personal. The Moment is powerful. And the best part is you have the power to turn any moment into The Moment.

To ensure The Moment isn't just a moment, but the start of something bigger, you must lock in The Mindset and The Meaning to make your changes permanent.

THE MINDSET

While many assume my primary focus is on refining players' on-court performance, a significant part of my work centers around shaping their mentality and boosting confidence.

One of the best examples of this was the first dinner I ever had with Tyrese Haliburton.

Tyrese's agent, Dave Spahn, called me and told me that Tyrese wanted to hire me to take his game to the next level because he was eligible for a contract extension after the following season.

I was traveling to Philadelphia to work with Joel Embiid the next week and Tyrese was going to be in town playing against him, so I told Dave to set up a dinner so we could all meet.

Tyrese was averaging 13.8 points per game at the time, which was way under what I thought he was capable of after breaking down his film.

During the two-hour dinner, we talked about what he wanted to accomplish throughout his career and what he needed to do to turn those aspirations into reality.

The biggest thing holding him back was his lack of scoring aggressiveness, so I presented a challenge to him. I told him that if he wanted to work with me, he had to have 14 field goal attempts the next night against the Sixers.

The result did not matter. Whether he made all 14 shots or missed every one of them, I was willing to take him on as a client as long as he took 14 shots during the game. If he attempted fewer than 14, I told him that I was not going to work with him moving forward.

The next night, Tyrese attempted 19 field goals and made 11 of them, en route to a career-high 38 points, which was 24 points more than his season average.

Tyrese thought he needed me to teach him new moves to improve his scoring, but what he really needed was for me to teach him a new mindset.

As promised, I took on Tyrese as a full-time client. All the time we dedicated to refining both his game and his mindset yielded significant returns the following season, as he secured his first All-Star selection and inked a lucrative $260 million max extension.

While incorporating new skills or enhancing existing ones can certainly help you reach a goal, sometimes a new mindset is the key ingredient that you have been missing.

BEING UNSELFISH CAN BE SELFISH

Encouraging a high school freshman to be more arrogant isn't a typical request, but that's exactly what I told Jayson Tatum he needed to do.

Initially, his mom wasn't entirely supportive of my suggestion because she wanted her son to be a humble star. However, everything changed during Jayson's junior year when his high school team was upset in the state semifinals.

During that game, Jayson sank 2 free throws to give

his team a 13-point lead with 4:48 remaining in the third quarter. Unfortunately, he only managed to score 3 points in the last 12 minutes and 12 seconds, while the other team went on a 30–14 run to close the game and advance to the finals.

Jayson was the best player in the country, but he watched his chance at winning his first state championship slip away instead of taking over the game like he was capable of.

After the game, his mom walked up to me and said something along the lines of, "Make him arrogant. Make him an asshole. Whatever you gotta do, do it, because I can't watch that happen ever again."

She was referring to Jayson's lack of aggressiveness. He was reluctant to speak up and insist that his teammates run the offense through him, because he didn't want to come across as selfish. He had to learn that *sometimes the most selfish thing to do is be unselfish.* Playing too unselfishly and not demanding the ball negatively impacted his team's chances of winning.

Jayson had an entirely different swagger the following postseason. He dominated and helped his team win their first five playoff games by an average of 32 points per game, securing a spot in the state championship.

The state championship game would be his last high school game and his last chance to hang a banner.

He demanded the ball from the jump and put on

a show. At halftime, Jayson had 27 points. The other team had 26. Jayson finished the game with 40 points in a convincing win that put an exclamation point on an amazing high school career.

Jayson had developed a quality shared by all great athletes, which I like to refer to as the "it" factor.

THE "IT" FACTOR

Michael Jordan had it. Serena Williams had it. Usain Bolt had it. Tiger Woods had it. And my mom has it. Oh yeah, my mom has it in spades.

What is the "it" I'm referring to? It's The Mindset to do whatever is required to get the job done. And there is no one, and I mean no one, that does whatever is needed to get the job done more than a loving parent.

While athletes, performers, and CEOs don't want to let their teammates, fans, or employees down, there is a different level of "I got you, I won't ever let you down" that a great parent has when it comes to being there for their children.

I saw it firsthand from both of my parents. My father spent long hours running a butcher shop in St. Louis. It was physically demanding, and while it was honest and steady work that put food on our table and a roof over our heads, my dad sacrificed a lot to give my siblings and me the best possible childhoods that he could.

My mom also dedicated her entire life to ensuring my sisters and I had everything she could possibly give us. When we couldn't afford to play on the best, select sports teams, she started cleaning houses for extra money so that we could play. Did she love scrubbing other people's toilets? Of course not. But she loved us and wanted the best for us, which meant doing whatever it took to provide the best opportunities for us.

When my family couldn't afford to send my sisters to the private high school they wanted to go to, she started shopping at garage sales to resell stuff on eBay to help pay for their tuition.

Did she like all the work that went into reselling these items? No way. But when my sisters said they wanted to attend St. Joseph's Academy, she figured out a way to make it happen.

MAMA MENTALITY

The most powerful display of what it means to be a great and fierce parent is the tough conversation my family had when we first discussed adopting my little sister Lulu.

Because of my grandma's close work with Melissa's Hope orphanage in Haiti, my family had hosted a few other amazing children who needed medical care before Lulu. My mom and dad loved hosting them while they were in the United States getting specialized treatments. After they completed their medical treatments, the children returned to their families, who were always so excited to have them back home.

We did the same with Lulu, who was an infant when she first came to stay with us. She stayed with us for almost a year as medical professionals inserted a shunt in her brain to treat her severe hydrocephalus and administered various medications to manage her seizures.

As soon as she was healthy enough, we brought Lulu back to her family in Haiti, who were anxiously awaiting her return. However, shortly after arriving in Haiti, her health began to decline, and her seizures worsened. She lost almost half the fifteen pounds she weighed in her first week home. Since the medical attention she desperately needed was not available in Haiti, her dad contacted my mom and asked if our family would consider adopting Lulu so that she could get the ongoing medical attention she needed. My mom knew that the only way to save her life was to bring her back to our home and begin the adoption process.

The only problem was the adoption process would take three to five years and there was no chance that Lulu would make it that long shuttling back and forth from Haiti to St. Louis. So my mom figured out a way to get an emergency medical visa to get her back in the States.

My family was eating dinner when my mom broke

the news. "We are adopting Lulu. She isn't getting the medical attention that she needs in Haiti, and we can help."

I remember my dad saying, "Colleen, how are we going to afford another child when we're tight on money as it is?"

And with the most awesome display of The Mindset that I've ever seen, my mom said, in her stubborn and sarcastic tone, "We will make it work. She needs us. She can eat my food. I don't need to eat. I'll be good."

There was nothing, absolutely nothing, that was going to stop my mom from helping Lulu.

This is what great athletes, performers, entrepreneurs, and, yes, parents, do. They don't let shit get in their way. If there is a wall in their way, no matter how high or how hard, they find a way to get around it, over it, under it, or they blast through it. They get past the fucking wall one way or another.

> THE GREAT ONES GET PAST
> THE FUCKING WALL
> ONE WAY OR ANOTHER.

Kobe Bryant called his mindset the "Mamba Mentality." I like to call my mom's mindset the "Mama Mentality."

No matter how sick or tired my mom was feeling or how much was on her plate, she was always there for us every day. Every day! There was not one morning when she woke up and said, "Not today, kids. Best of luck. I'm taking the day off."

The Mindset is about doing what needs to be done, regardless if you feel like doing it or not. There are a lot of people who say they're willing to do whatever it takes to make it happen until it's time to do whatever it takes to make it happen.

That's what separates the greats from the wannabes, the average, and the people who settle instead of doing whatever is required to reach their full potential.

There were plenty of days that Michael Jordan, Serena Williams, Usain Bolt, and Tiger Woods didn't feel like eating well, stretching, working out, watching film, etc. But they understood that doing those things repeatedly at a high level, especially when you don't want to, is how you win.

It's the unwavering commitment to doing what must be done, regardless of the obstacles that may arise and the inner resistance that may surface, that you need to apply to your own life if you want to win as well.

Having the right Mindset helps you win the battles in your head.

Now you need The Meaning to win the battles in your heart.

THE MEANING

My grandpa Papa Dink was my biggest fan. He never missed a game and would brag about me to anyone who would listen.

Papa Dink was also a superhard worker who was a second-generation butcher and spent all day on his feet and using his hands. He took a ton of pride in caring for his customers, but over the years, his body ached more and more at the end of every day due to the long hours of physically challenging work.

In true Irish form, he felt the best way to get rid of those aches and pains was to enjoy a few whiskeys on the rocks. Unfortunately, decisions like that have consequences, and Papa Dink's drinking eventually led to liver failure and his passing in 2010.

While I focus on remembering all the amazing qualities of Papa Dink, I wish he had chosen a better remedy for his pain. I'm sure if he knew all those drinks would rob him of a chance to watch me play in two NCAA tournaments, he would have done a lot less drinking at night.

Like Papa Dink, so many of us make choices without adequately thinking about the consequences of our actions until they pile up beyond our control.

Papa Dink didn't realize a few drinks would cost him a decade of great memories with his soulmate, Grandma

Lee, and the rest of his family. He was just trying to solve an immediate problem with a short-term solution, not realizing that dulling those aches and pains would lead to an even bigger problem over time.

People only change when they are *emotionally compelled to,* which is why you must connect to the things that matter most to you.

> PEOPLE ONLY CHANGE WHEN THEY ARE EMOTIONALLY COMPELLED TO, WHICH IS WHY YOU MUST CONNECT TO THE THINGS THAT MATTER MOST TO YOU.

Are you driven by making money, having the best possible marriage, passing the bar exam, driving a Porsche, or doing whatever it takes to compete in an Iron Man triathlon? Regardless of what you're after, you must make sure you understand exactly why you want it in the first place.

If you can't clearly and concisely articulate The Meaning and reasons behind your desires and goals, you're setting yourself up for a higher probability of failure.

Get clear on this point. Before you make any decision, you must understand why you are making that decision and the results from the decision you make.

WHAT'S YOUR REASON?

Choosing to eat tacos, a burger, or a salad for lunch is not that big of a deal. It's only one meal, right? But if you're tired of feeling sluggish and overweight, or you've had health problems because of a poor diet, then the meaning of your decision becomes more significant. Salads make sense if you're trying to improve your long-term health or physique, while cheeseburgers and tacos make sense if you're looking for a convenient meal to cure your immediate hunger.

It should come as no surprise that nearly 80 percent of New Year's resolutions last less than a month. Why? Because people usually don't attach enough meaning to their decisions. Their resolutions are fueled by a motivational moment instead of a compelling emotional meaning. These people have created a huge uphill climb before they even started.

If I had to guess, the people who failed to keep their New Year's resolutions were probably the same people who spent all of November and December telling all their friends about their plans to make positive changes on January 1 and couldn't wait until the ball dropped at midnight to tweet #NewYearNewMe.

Anyone who can impact and improve their life now, but chooses to wait for a new year, a birthday, or a holiday to start, doesn't have enough passion and meaning attached to that decision. Decisions without those things are doomed to fail.

By themselves, willpower and good intentions will only take you so far. Both are subject to external distractions that knock you off your game plan. You need both, but they are only supporting players. Willpower and good intentions are finite, which is why we have a better chance of succeeding by linking a powerful emotional reason to our goal.

To succeed, you must have an intense internal emotional component that drives you. And that intense emotional component is called meaning.

WHY DO YOU WANT TO CHANGE?

You may be a highly analytical person who doesn't like to explore your mindset, meanings, and emotions, but to stop bullshitting yourself, you must confront these aspects head-on.

MAKE IT MEAN MORE

A few years back, I was on a flight when I came across research that linked obesity to a shorter life expectancy. While it's obvious that the healthier you are, the longer you'll usually live, this study had a chart detailing exactly how many years of life you were expected to lose based on how overweight you are.

This caught my eye because, like my grandpa, my dad works as a butcher and chef. He always joked, "You can't trust a skinny chef," and he sported a belly as big as his heart. (He has a BIG heart!) Anytime we tried to tell him to eat better or workout more, he'd tell us that he didn't care what he looked like and would rather enjoy good barbecue and beer than salads and water.

While I didn't care about what my dad's body *looked* like, I did care if one of the people I loved most was alive and healthy. I knew my dad was setting himself up for failure later in life if he didn't make immediate changes.

However, until this research, I didn't know just how bad the future was looking for my dad. I found his weight and height on the chart and saw that, on average, a person of his size lost six years of life due to obesity.

It was time for him to make a change. But to help him want to make that change, I didn't need to educate him. I needed to touch his heart. He knew he was overweight. He just didn't care enough to do anything about it.

I met him in the driveway when he got home from work one night. Before he could even say hello, I started an hour-long conversation with him by saying, "Do you want to be there for your grandkids? Do you want to be there for us? Or do you want us to miss you every day because you were too selfish to get yourself in shape?"

The next day, my dad woke up an hour before work and walked for the first time. I still remember how proud and happy I was when I received the sweaty selfie he sent after completing his walk. My dad still didn't care how he looked, but when he realized that losing those extra pounds would mean more time with his family, he set his alarm, laced up his shoes, walked out the door, and exercised for the first time in years.

He stayed with it, quickly gaining more energy and physically feeling better. Most important, he was proud of his efforts, especially after he lost almost ninety pounds in a year.

If you're struggling to add meaning to your decisions, consider writing a letter to your future self, something along these lines.

Dear Me,

You're in pain on your deathbed right now because you refused to eat well, work out, and put down the alcohol. If you had eaten better, walked around the block every night, and decided to only drink responsibly on special occasions, you'd be enjoying a family barbecue, a day in the park, or a movie night with the people you love right now.

Instead, you're in the hospital and going to die soon. Because you didn't make the right decisions, you'll miss two of your grandchildren's weddings and one of their graduations.

On top of that, your family and friends must live with the pain of missing you. All because you decided to make bad choices along the way. Why didn't you think about the costs when you were doing these things?

Sincerely,

Me

The more specific you get, the more it will hit your heart. Paint the picture of your life if you don't take the action you know you need to take. Think about the things that you're doing or not doing and what will eventually happen because of those decisions.

If you keep coming home miserable from work and letting your work life negatively impact your personal life, how will that work out for you and your family in the long run? How much are you hurting yourself and your career by settling for a job that doesn't challenge you or pay you as much as you think you're worth? Do you want to be a fun and active grandparent later

> THE TIME TO FIX THE ROOF ISN'T WHEN IT'S RAINING. AND THE TIME TO FIX YOUR LIFE ISN'T WHEN IT'S COMPLETELY BROKEN.

in life or constantly deal with pain and medical problems that were mostly preventable?

The time to fix the roof isn't when it's raining. And the time to fix your life isn't when it's completely broken.

It sucks when people wait to make changes until they have to instead of taking proactive steps to prevent problems in the first place. You need to think and believe positive changes aren't optional. They are essential.

If crystal balls were real and you could see clearly into the future, you would start making changes today. Absent that, you need to get to a place where you realize just how much the weight—literal or figurative—

A LETTER TO YOUR FUTURE SELF

you're holding on to is holding you down. You must also acknowledge that while the tendency is to blame external forces, often the thing that is holding you down the most is you.

MORE MEANING, MORE ACTION

Jack Wiemar was just under six feet tall but weighed nearly three hundred pounds.

He frequently visited the doctor due to his struggle with obesity and his doctor kept telling him that he wasn't going to live very long unless he started dieting and working out to get back down to a healthy weight.

His doctor feared he was on a path to die of a heart attack or stroke.

While Jack didn't like being obese and would have loved to have a better body, he never was committed or disciplined enough to actually make it happen.

And then one day, he got bad news that his daughter Megan had been diagnosed with a rare kidney disease. Her doctors said she needed a kidney transplant so the first thing they did was test everyone in the family to see if anyone was a potential match to provide a kidney to save her.

They waited for the results, hoping that one of them would be able to help her out. Turns out, Jack was a perfect match. He was not only willing to donate his kidney but excited that he was going to be able to help his daughter.

But there was a problem. The doctors refused to operate on him because he was too obese and they feared they might lose him during the procedure.

He was devastated.

If he would have taken his health more seriously, he could have saved his daughter. But because he made poor choices, he wasn't in a position to do so. He was still determined to help. He asked the doctors how much time his daughter had before she absolutely needed a kidney. They told him maybe six months.

Over the next six months, Jack, now motivated by an extremely important meaning, lost one hundred pounds. He donated one of his kidneys to his daughter, ultimately saving her life.

For years, he'd wanted to shed those extra pounds, but it never meant enough to him. But the second his daughter's life was on the line, he suddenly had more than enough motivation and meaning to take action.

Maybe you are just like Jack.

Maybe it's not that you're incapable of doing the things you've always wanted to do but have struggled to do to this point. Maybe it's just that you've never had a powerful enough emotional reason to take action.

USE MOTIVATION TO START AND MEANING TO FINISH

You can figure out your meaning and attach a powerful emotion to it, but still not act. You may be motivated, which is where all changes and decisions start. But unless you attach meaning, you'll have a hard time crossing the finish line.

When you're equipped with all the essential information but still find yourself hesitating to make a decision, it's likely due to a lack of mental toughness to choose the right course of action. In this scenario, the obstacle has shifted from a gap in knowledge to an action gap, preventing you from taking the decisive steps needed to move forward.

That's where discipline comes in. You may not think of discipline as an emotion, but it is. For many people, it's an uncomfortable emotion, which is why so many of us avoid it.

Our analytical brain can tell us where we should go, but our emotional brain has the driver's wheel and ultimately decides where we're going.

Take the simple act of eating a piece of cake.

The only way you can win this battle in your mind is if you convince your emotional brain that it's a good idea not to eat the cake. Your thinking brain can tell you that cake is bad for you, but your emotional brain tells you cake tastes great! It convinces you that one piece won't kill you, especially if you've consistently worked out and you're looking for a reward.

That's why tying emotional reasons, including discipline, to solving your problems is so important. You won't take a bite if you're disciplined, no matter how good that cake is, the occasion, or who baked it.

Next time you're faced with a decision and trying

THE BIGGER THE "WHY,"
THE EASIER THE "HOW."

to figure out *how* to stay disciplined, shift your thinking and figure out *why* you should remain disciplined. It's the difference between attaching a process and attaching meaning.

The bigger the "why," the easier the "how." If the "why" is big enough, you can overcome any size of "how."

Here's the ultimate example of "how" versus "why" thinking.

My high school classmate John McLain was a skinny, 120-pound freshman on the basketball team. One day, his uncle crawled under a car to work on it.

The jack wasn't secured properly and the car fell on him, crushing every bit of air out of his body.

Nobody is quite sure how he did it, but John somehow single-handedly managed to lift that car long enough for his uncle to start breathing again. He begged his uncle to move, but the car had broken countless bones in his body. John had to hold that car up until his dad helped him move the car aside, saving his uncle's life.

The "why" of saving his uncle's life far outstripped the "how" he could deadlift the car until his uncle was safe.

Where there's a will, there's a way.

When you look at where you are in life, you will see the decisions you made in the past have led to the life you're currently living.

The decision to go on a first date can lead to the amazing relationship you're in now or the unhealthy relationship that drained you before you ended it in an ugly fashion. Deciding to change jobs and taking the first thing you're offered may land you your dream job, but it could also put you in a company you dread working for every day. Taking out a huge car loan for the ride of your dreams may not be the smartest idea if you can't afford the insurance, upkeep, and hefty car payments.

Every decision you make steers your life in a different direction for better or worse.

The decisions you make sculpt your life and are based on opportunities or challenges that come into your life all the time. You must formulate the right criteria for the decisions you make instead of acting selfishly or impulsively. Short-term thinking can end up being long-term pain with a healthy dose of regret added on.

This isn't to say that if you think the right way, you'll always make the right decisions. But when your thinking is sound, and things don't turn out the way you hoped, you can rest easy knowing that you made your best attempt given what you had to work with at the time.

• • •

Now that you know how to create The Moment, develop The Mindset, and increase The Meaning, it's time for you to make The Decision.

Are you ready to make today "Day One," or will you allow the bullshit to continue and keep saying, "One day"? If you want it bad enough, you'll make today "Day One." If you don't, you'll keep telling yourself, "One day."

Put yourself in The Moment. Be aware of the right mindset you'll need. And then attach a powerful meaning to it.

All that's left is for you to make your decision.

THE BLUEPRINT

When you open the Uber app, there is an important question in the center of the screen: "Where to?" Just to the right, you're prompted to decide whether you want to go now or schedule a time for later. Both are simple yet significant choices.

Now, I pose the same questions to you: "Where to?" Where do you want to go in life, and are you ready to go now? Unlike Uber, no one will pick you up and take you to your destination in life. The good news is you're in the driver's seat, with the freedom to go wherever your heart desires.

The Blueprint is designed to help you pinpoint exactly where you want to go and construct a road map to get you there.

THE DESTINATION

Figuring out where you want to go in life can feel just as hard as the journey itself.

I have a proven way to solve that problem for you. It's a process I've used with my NBA clients for over a decade now that will help you pinpoint where you want to go and give you a step-by-step blueprint to get there.

The goal of this book isn't to simply motivate or educate you, but to also activate you. So instead of telling you how to build The Blueprint, we're going to build your blueprint together.

You started this process in The Audit, where you looked back at the bullshit that already exists in your life. In The Gap, you took stock of the discrepancy between where you are and where you want to be. With The Decision, you found your "why" for closing this gap. The Blueprint is *how* you're going to close it.

The first step of The Blueprint is to do a brain dump and list all the things in your life you want or need to change. This is different from The Audit because now you're looking forward instead of to the past and the present. This exercise may take fifteen minutes, or it may take several days depending on your personality type, how thorough you are, and the number of things you want to work on.

If you're like most, there are probably a ton of things you want to improve, and I want you to list them all.

LIST THE THINGS YOU WANT TO IMPROVE IN YOUR LIFE:

☐ _____

☐ _____

☐ _____

☐ _____

☐ _____

After listing everything that you want, rank them in order of importance. Chances are there will be several big-ticket items tied to your health, career, relationships, and more.

While improving all the things on your list can certainly improve your well-being, it's impossible to improve them all at the same time, which is why it's important to rank them in order of importance. If you try to take all of them on simultaneously, you'll fracture your attention into a million pieces and won't have the dedicated energy you need to fix the most important thing on your list.

You may be thinking, "How do I choose one thing?" Don't overcomplicate your answer. The question I always ask is, "If you could only improve one thing in your life, which one would have the greatest impact on your well-being?"

Where will you see the greatest and most important return on your emotional, time, and energy investment? Again, it's okay if you don't have an immediate answer. Your decision is going to result in a serious commitment.

Listen to both your gut and your heart. Be honest! Don't take the easy way out! Take on the biggest challenge where the biggest deficit exists in your life. You can either take a half-hearted approach and get mediocre results, or you can display some grit and get important shit done. You choose, but do so knowing there are consequences to faking your answers and rankings.

Take your first list and rework it so that your priorities are in order.

> *PRIORITIZE THE THINGS YOU WANT TO IMPROVE IN YOUR LIFE:*
>
> 1 _____
>
> 2 _____
>
> 3 _____
>
> 4 _____
>
> 5 _____

There you go. Now you're getting somewhere!

THE CHANGE

The next step is one you might not like, but it's one of the most beneficial things I do with all my NBA clients and the executives who I work with. Circle your top priority and draw a line through every other item on your list. This now becomes known as The Change.

I know, I know. The bullshit is starting to creep in again. I can hear it now. "But wait, those things are im-

IDENTIFY THE CHANGE YOU
WANT TO MAKE IN YOUR LIFE:

(1)

2

3

4

5

portant too." Yes, they are. But not right now. Set them aside for the time being. Your top priority is a whopper, and you'll need every ounce of energy and focus you have to meet it head-on.

Trying to change several things at once will lead you down a path of feeling depleted and defeated. Think of developing your blueprint like playing a game of chess because the way you win in life is also the way you win in chess.

Chess is a game of priorities. Out of many different potential plans, the successful player must select the one path that is the most promising and the most essential, and then work toward it over the course of many moves, despite the obstacles their opponent throws at them.

Our modern-day, multitasking selves are the enemy of this kind of thinking. We're so bombarded from all directions today that the word "priority" turned into "priorities" long ago. Of course you still have responsibilities in many areas, but for your purposes, you should only have one priority when you're developing your blueprint.

I know a lot of you are wired to complete as many tasks as possible. I've seen your to-do lists, and I know for a fact that even on your best days, weeks, and months there's no way you're completing even a fraction of what's on them. Worse yet, hyper-sized lists like this distract you and suck energy away from the few things that matter most. And that's what we're trying to avoid. That's why you need to circle your priority and cross out everything else.

Now that you know The Change you want to make, it's time to build The Blueprint to bring it to life. Before you do, there's one important ground rule to keep in mind: *The better the details, the better The Blueprint.*

How detailed should you be? As detailed as a regular at Starbucks. I'm not a coffee drinker, but I'm always blown away by the level of detail that Starbucks customers use when they order. They don't just ask for a coffee. They order a *Venti, light-iced, skinny, sugar-free hazelnut macchiato with an extra shot and no whipped cream.*

You need to apply that same level of detail to your blueprint.

BLUEPRINT BUBBLES

To start building your blueprint, we're going to create an easy-to-use organizer that I call Blueprint Bubbles.

Write The Change you want to make in the top bubble.

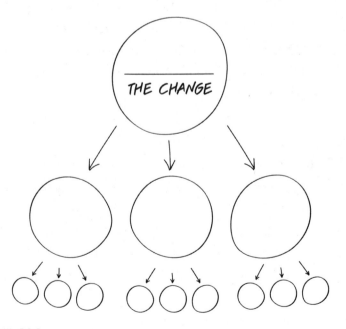

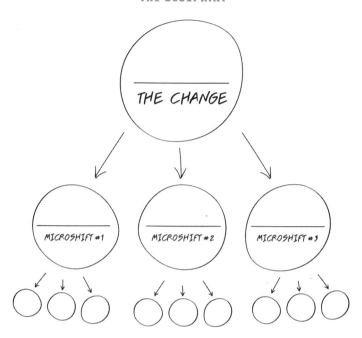

Next, identify three primary shifts you need to make for The Change to become a reality. I like to call these MicroShifts because they don't have to be big changes to have big impacts.

For example, if The Change you want to make is to lose weight, your three MicroShifts may be to eat healthier, be more active, and sleep better. Suppose The Change you want to make is to improve your financial situation. Your three MicroShifts may be working more, spending less, and adding additional revenue streams. When The Change you want to make is to be less stressed, your three MicroShifts may be to spend more time doing activities you enjoy, eliminating negative energy from your environment, and creating a Not-to-Do List. (More on that later).

Take some time to lock in on the three MicroShifts you're going to make, then write them on the second line of the Blueprint Bubbles.

Next, you need to dig down to the next level of each MicroShift to pinpoint the three actions to take related to that shift. Remember, details matter! Be as specific as possible.

For example, if your change is to lose weight, your first MicroShift may be to eat healthier. That's a great shift to make, but you need to identify exactly how to eat healthier. You may choose to avoid desserts, fast between 8 P.M. and 10 A.M., and only drink water.

To be more active, you may choose to take the stairs instead of the elevator in your office building or apartment complex, do a thirty-minute workout every morning, and go on a nightly walk around the neighborhood.

You might accomplish the third MicroShift of sleeping better by eliminating technology thirty minutes before bed, setting a 10 P.M. bedtime, and buying a new mattress or pillow that helps you fall asleep faster and sleep more soundly.

Again, these don't have to be massive actions. But they must be actions you will actually take. They should be meaningful and challenging but not to the point you make them so difficult you'll never accomplish them consistently. This is why it's okay to schedule in a thirty-minute workout every morning but not a three-hour workout at the end of a long day. Building MicroShift victories feeds into the positive momentum you can draw upon when needed.

Think through actions that will help you accomplish your MicroShifts and write them in the third line of bubbles on the previous page.

Your Blueprint Bubbles don't have to stop after three layers. You can keep adding layers until you have itemized all the details you need to give you the best chance at making The Change.

For instance, if you listed that you're going to do a morning workout, you could easily add another layer of bubbles and list the exact time, where, and what you're going to do for that workout. Taking it one step further, you could also add another layer and break out individual workouts by day on a rotation basis. Monday is leg day. Tuesday is cardio day. Wednesday is a Pilates class or spin workout, and so forth.

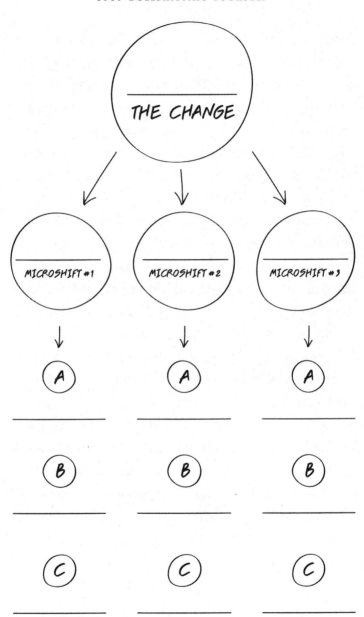

STARTER STEPS

Once we complete our Blueprint Bubbles, it's time to figure out the Starter Step for each action that we want to take.

What is a Starter Step? A short, simple, and attainable action to help you get started.

Why are Starter Steps important? Because time and time again, people set lofty goals only to abandon them after a few days or worse, never start. If you've ever set an ambitious New Year's resolution and then not followed through with it, you know exactly what I mean.

People who attempt complicated, life-altering changes without breaking those challenges into small steps end up right back where they started or worse, because now they feel like a failure for falling short again.

The goal of the Blueprint Bubbles is to break down The Blueprint into small and attainable actions you can and will actually do. Simply put, the easier and more straightforward something is to do, the more likely you will do it. The harder and more complicated something is to do, the less likely you will do it.

Change is not rocket science, yet people mess this part up and overwhelm themselves unnecessarily when trying to make changes in their life. Starting small is better than not starting at all, which is why Starter Steps are a key part of your approach.

For example, what's a good Starter Step if you want to run a marathon for the first time? Start by jogging around the block tomorrow morning. While that jog isn't going to prepare you for the 26.2 miles you'll eventually conquer, it will start the habit of running, which is what you are after. Maybe not tomorrow or the day after that, but when you feel great after circling the block, keep running!

Want a cleaner house? Start by tidying up one room. While that isn't going to get you ready to host a party, it will get you a little closer to having your home in order. And if you still have energy after that first room, keep cleaning!

Starter Steps get you going. Keep them small. Because if the first step is too big, you may never take it. Build momentum and consistency. Gradually increase intensity and difficulty as you level up. You're beginning the process of replacing old habits that don't serve you well with new ones that do. That's why there are several levels to Blueprint Bubbles. They are specifically built to

encourage accomplishments. Remember, details should be as small and as focused as needed. Starter Steps are specifically designed to reinforce that idea.

If you find yourself struggling with consistency, lower the intensity and difficulty to restore momentum. If momentum is lost altogether, revert to Starter Steps until you regain confidence and consistency. It's a gradual process of building positive habits and achieving small victories that add up to big wins.

STACKING THE DECK

Now that you have an action plan and Starter Steps, it's time to stack the deck. In this step, you'll arrange the elements of your blueprint in a favorable way to achieve the result you want.

Stacking the deck can be as small as laying out clothes the night before to help you run in the morning, food prepping to help you maintain your healthy eating, or volunteering as a coach because you want to be actively involved in your kids' lives.

The reason stacking the deck works is that human beings tend to be pretty lazy. When you stack the deck in your favor, you can use laziness to your advantage by making the most beneficial choices also the easiest choices. You'll be amazed at how much of an advantage you can gain by stacking the deck, even just a little bit.

Deleting your ex's contact info in your phone is the difference between you drunk-texting them and you maintaining your dignity when your change involves starting a new life after a nasty breakup.

Taping a notecard to the honey buns in your cabinet that says, *You have to run for 30 minutes to burn off these 290 calories,* can be the difference between you pigging out and sticking to your diet.

Leaving your debit card in your hotel room instead of carrying it in your wallet at the blackjack tables in Las Vegas is literally stacking the deck in your favor. If you've got a gambling problem that you want to change, this is the difference between you losing a little cash or emptying out your bank account trying to get back to even with a hot streak that never comes. Trust me, I learned this one the hard way, and I know I'm not alone.

Yes, you can still ask a friend for your ex's number, chow down the honey buns, or go grab your debit card to withdraw more money, but the added effort to do those things will make it less likely that you do them. What you're doing is creating barriers that are big enough to make you stop and think about why you want to stop bull-shitting yourself.

Ultimately, if you want to do any of these things and put yourself farther away from The Change, nobody can stop you. As I've said repeatedly already, it's up to you and nobody else. How bad do you want a new and better life? You decide.

Stacking the deck creates an environment that encourages desirable behaviors while making undesirable ones difficult to pursue. By making beneficial choices easy and accessible and undesirable choices difficult and inconvenient, you are setting yourself up for success.

SUCCESS STRATEGIES

I want to give you four additional strategies to raise the chances of you taking action.

The first is **Linking**.

Linking is when you connect a new behavior to an existing behavior.

My dad used Linking when he lost ninety pounds in a single year. He was not a fan of exercising but loved

DESIRED BEHAVIOR:

1 _____

2 _____

3 _____

4 _____

5 _____

LINKING WITH EXISTING BEHAVIOR:

1 _____

2 _____

3 _____

4 _____

5 _____

listening to sports podcasts and his favorite rock band, AC/DC. He decided to link the two and made a deal with himself that he could only listen to them when he was walking. While he still hated walking, he enjoyed the podcasts and his favorite songs enough to do it daily.

The second is **Checks and Xs.**

Checks and Xs is when you use your calendar to document your progress, good and bad.

Let's say you want to read a book. You set a goal of reading ten pages a day. At the end of each day, if you read ten pages or more, you get to put a big green check on that day. If you read less than ten pages, you put a big red X on that day.

Those big red Xs will haunt you and make you feel bad, so you'll usually do anything you can to avoid them, which ultimately encourages the actions you want to take.

The third is **Empty the Jar**.

I've used this strategy with some of my NBA clients. One of them wanted to shoot more three-pointers, so we set a goal of attempting at least 500 three-pointers during the season. That works out to a little over 7 threes per game if he played in 85 percent of his team's games.

We put two jars in his locker. One jar had five hundred marbles in it, while the other had none. After each game, he moved one marble from the full jar to the other jar for every three-pointer he attempted. The goal was to empty the jar that started with five hundred marbles. That season he shot over 550 threes, which was double the number he had shot the previous season.

The fourth is **Benchmark Bingo**.

This strategy turns your to-do list into a Bingo game that you can play with your coworkers or an accountability buddy. Each square on the Bingo card represents a specific task or milestone that needs to be completed within a designated time frame. As you finish each task, mark it on your Bingo card. The first person to complete a Bingo (a full row, column, or diagonal streak) wins a reward.

BENCHMARK BINGO

B	I	N	G	O
CLOSE A POLICY WITH A NEW CLIENT	SET 20 NEW APPOINTMENTS IN A WEEK	GET REFERRED/ ENDORSED TO 5 A+ PROSPECTS IN A WEEK	MAINTAIN A PROACTIVE REBALANCING STRATEGY FOR CLIENTS	PARTICIPATE IN A TEAM TRAINING SESSION
ACHIEVE A 20% INCREASE IN MONTHLY PREMIUM TARGETS	ESTABLISH A STRATEGIC PARTNERSHIP WITH A LOCAL BUSINESS FOR REFERRALS	SUCCESSFULLY CROSS-SELL ADDITIONAL COVERAGE	SUCCESSFULLY UPSELL A LONG-TERM CARE POLICY TO EXISTING CLIENTS	SECURE A POLICY RENEWAL WITH AN UPSELL
CLOSE A POLICY WITH A HIGH COVERAGE VALUE	REVIEW TAX LAWS TO STAY UP TO DATE	DEVELOP AND EXECUTE A REFERRAL REWARDS PROGRAM FOR CLIENTS	ATTEND A NETWORKING EVENT	HOST A VIRTUAL WORKSHOP ON RETIREMENT PLANNING
EXCEED 50 WEEKLY OUTBOUND CALLS TARGET	CREATE AND SHARE A WEEKLY EMAIL NEWSLETTER WITH CLIENTS	LEAD A LUNCH-AND-LEARN SESSION FOR TEAM KNOWLEDGE SHARING	CREATE A NEW SALES PITCH FOR A SPECIFIC POLICY TYPE	DEVELOP A CREATIVE MARKETING CAMPAIGN FOR A POLICY TYPE
ESTABLISH A MULTI-GENERATIONAL CLIENTELE	MAINTAIN 95% RETENTION ON ASSETS UNDER MANAGEMENT	SUCCESSFULLY RESOLVE THREE CLIENT COMPLAINTS OR CONCERNS IN A MONTH	COMPLETE A CONTINUING EDUCATION COURSE	MEET WITH 5 PROSPECTIVE CLIENTS FACE-TO-FACE IN A WEEK

Accountability visuals are awesome when used the right way. Even something as simple as posting sticky notes on your bathroom mirror or changing your phone lock screen can help motivate you to follow through on your commitments.

WOULD YOU BET ON YOU?

Now that you've completed The Blueprint and have actionable steps to take and strategies to help you follow through, I have a question for you.

Would you bet on you?

Would you bet on yourself to follow through and actually make The Change through the necessary several layers of MicroShifts? Are you willing to bet everything in your bank account on The Change you decided to make for yourself? If you want to raise the stakes even more, would you let the person you love most bet their life savings on you? Or would you tell them to save their money because you're worried you might fail?

Your answer to these questions says a lot about your confidence in and commitment to strengthening your ability to improve your life.

Maybe you're cautious because you've let yourself down in the past. Perhaps you're afraid to get your hopes up because you don't want to feel like shit if it doesn't work out. Or you're afraid to go all in because you fear giving The Change your best attempt, and your best may still not be good enough.

Whatever it is that's messing with your head, you need to let it go. You built The Blueprint you needed. You know exactly what to do.

Now go do it.

THE WORK

You can figure out what your bullshit is, analyze where you're falling short, and even make a detailed plan to attack the problem. But it doesn't amount to anything, unless you put in The Work!

By now, you should have eliminated all the bullshit excuses and reasons why you haven't started in the past. Filtering out as much of the bullshit as possible will give you the confidence, clarity, and direction you need to finally start doing The Work.

It's all about following through with action because The Blueprint only works if you do.

KNOWING VS. DOING

Plenty of people *know* they need to turn their life around, but it's a whole different story to actually *do* something to turn it around. If you're really ready to improve your life, you need to get to work. It's that simple.

Don't wait for the perfect time to start, or you'll be waiting forever. There is no better time to start than right now. You have The Blueprint, now you just have to put in The Work. Don't beat yourself up if you're still struggling to get started. You're not alone. In fact, this is where most people get tripped up.

Circle back to the Starter Steps you identified in The Blueprint. Remember, Starter Steps are short, simple actions you can easily accomplish to help you get started. Think of them as the kindling and matches you need to start your fire.

These actions are purposely easy to do because as you well know from accomplishing other things in your life, once you get started, it's a lot easier to keep going.

If you're still struggling to get started, review your Starter Steps and break them down into even easier actions. Go as deep as you need to until you find a place where you know you can get going. If you've thought about the other things the right way, you'll find the right level of detail that will trigger you into action.

If, after breaking down your Starter Steps into the smallest possible actions, you still can't get going, then something else is getting in the way. Is there an obstacle you need to remove, or are *you* the obstacle? Be honest. Your new life depends on it.

Are you telling yourself that a lack of time is holding you back? Well, it's not. You get the same number of hours in a day as everyone else. You simply need to adjust your priorities.

When you claim that a lack of money is the obstacle, start budgeting better or find alternate sources of income to improve your finances. People with fewer financial resources than you have been able to succeed despite their initial disadvantage, simply because they refused to let it be a roadblock.

If a lack of confidence is the obstacle, shrink your doubts into smaller actions you confidently know you can handle. Instead of walking a mile a day to start a new exercise regimen, do a lap around a short block near your home.

Regardless of the obstacle, you must find any way that you can to remove it so you can start making the change you're after. I've shown you how to remove excuses, so excuses are no longer acceptable.

THE UNSEEN HOURS

#NobodysGonnaKnow was a viral TikTok trend that amassed over two billion views. TikTokers made videos of themselves doing deceitful things when no one was watching, acting as if nobody would notice what they were doing.

These videos all used a viral audio clip that featured a dialogue between two people discussing their actions—

"Nobody's gonna know. Nobody's gonna know"—to which a second person responds, "They're gonna know." The first person then responds, "How would they know?"

Unfortunately, this isn't just a TikTok trend. This is how a lot of people live their lives. They try to play everyone else and end up playing themselves.

Nobody's gonna know all the work you do or don't do, but *they're gonna know* the results that you get. The evidence will be obvious one way or the other.

People won't know if you never miss a workout or skip them all. They won't know if you go hard during drills or half-ass them, or whether you pushed yourself during weights or simply got through the exercises. But they will see the improvements you make or don't make.

This is the essence of The Unseen Hours.

I coined this phrase years ago during an interview when I was asked what separates successful athletes, entrepreneurs, and high achievers from everyone else. There are a lot of factors that contribute to success in anything you try, but one of the biggest keys is mastering The Unseen Hours.

First-time marathon runners don't just wake up, lace up their running shoes, and head to the starting line. They prepare for months before, eliminating bad food from their diet and running hundreds of miles at shorter distances to build up their endurance. They hit the gym to increase core and leg strength and run 10K's or half-marathons to prepare for the full marathon. Crossing a marathon finish line comes from the countless Unseen Hours leading up to the day of the race.

Students who earn PhDs don't just show up and pass an exam. They spend many thousands of Unseen Hours attending classes, researching, and studying, meeting with professors and experts, writing their thesis, rewriting their thesis, and demonstrating mastery of the subject they're pursuing.

If you want to fully appreciate how a life is impacted when someone does the hard work in The Unseen Hours, talk to someone who has beaten a bad addiction. There were plenty of days they felt like giving up or giving in, but they stayed strong, shook off temptation, and are living healthier because of it.

It's easy to work hard and do the right thing when a bunch of eyes are on you, but what you do when no one is watching is where the real magic happens. So, the next time you're thinking about cheating The Work because no one is watching, know you're only cheating yourself.

> WHAT YOU DO WHEN NO ONE IS WATCHING IS WHERE THE REAL MAGIC HAPPENS.

Although no one else will know that you're cheating, you will know. You'll deny and rationalize your actions. But make no mistake . . . *you will know.*

Not only will you have to live with a lesser outcome from cheating or skipping The Work, but you'll also have to live with regret, knowing you let yourself down.

SLEEP OR SUCCESS?

In high school, Chamillionaire's "Good Morning" started playing on my phone every morning at 4:59 A.M. I picked that song as my wake-up call. It was an upbeat song with cocky lyrics, so it was the perfect song to get me in the right mood before my morning workout. I usually let it play for a little before turning off my alarm. It just became part of my morning routine.

Another reason why I let it play was so that I could read my alarm, which always said, *Sleep or Success . . . You Choose.*

There was no chance I was going to read that, then hit the snooze button and choose to go back to sleep instead of doing the work in my Unseen Hours. After Chamillionaire's chorus played for the second time, I would hop out of bed, brush my teeth, put on clothes, and head to the gym.

My high school principal, Jon Clark, met me in the gym at five-fifteen so I could go through my morning routine, which included shooting more than a thousand three-pointers.

I did the exact same routine every morning for four

years straight. Throughout my high school career, there were only four days that I didn't do my morning routine (three due to snow days and one due to illness), which means I shot approximately 1.5 million shots while the majority of my opponents were sleeping.

There were plenty of days I woke up tired, sore, or just didn't feel like getting out of bed. But there wasn't one time I regretted going to the gym and working out after I was finished. The Work wasn't always fun; in fact, a lot of times it sucked. But the results were always worth it.

All of those shots I practiced in an empty gym paid off. They helped my team win a state championship in high school. I was offered dozens of Division 1 scholarships. I chose Belmont University in Nashville, and in my senior year in college, I shot 48.2 percent from behind the three-point line. It is still one of the best three-point shooting seasons in NCAA history.

My success wasn't an accident, and it wasn't luck. *Success never is.*

While everyone else was sleeping, I was working on perfecting my jump shot. I figured out long ago that anything you accomplish in your life is directly attributable to the amount of quality work you put into it. It's a lesson you need to embed into your mindset too.

That's the thing I love about The Unseen Hours. While no one sees all the choices you make, or the work you put in behind closed doors when you're by yourself, they'll see the results and outcomes you get from those actions.

> WHILE NO ONE SEES ALL THE CHOICES YOU MAKE, OR THE WORK YOU PUT IN BEHIND CLOSED DOORS WHEN YOU'RE BY YOURSELF, THEY'LL SEE THE RESULTS AND OUTCOMES YOU GET FROM THOSE ACTIONS.

PILLOWS AND PARKING LOTS

Late one night many years ago, there was a knock on my car window followed by a stern voice that said, "Sir, you can't park here."

It was hotel security telling me I wasn't allowed to sleep in my car in their parking lot for safety reasons. This wasn't the first night or the only night that I slept in my car while on the road.

I wasn't homeless, but at the start of my training career, I drove around the Midwest running clinics and camps with anyone who would partner with me. Most events I charged $20 per player, so if they sold out, I made a grand or two. At other clinics for private teams, I was only making a couple hundred bucks.

On the days when I only made $200 or $300, it didn't seem smart to spend half of it on a hotel room, so I would just park in the darkest spot I could find and hope no one noticed me.

Flashing back to moments like this makes me appreciate even more all the hard work and sacrifices I made to get to where I am today.

During those early years, I wore a band on my wrist that said *Sacrifice Now. Succeed Later.* Back then, I just thought it was catchy. Now I realize how important the wisdom of those four little words is.

To succeed at anything, you're going to have to sacrifice. Sometimes that means sleeping in your car to save a few bucks. It could mean bypassing partying in your twenties to build the business of your dreams. Or changing careers to a more family-friendly schedule because you want to be the best spouse and parent possible.

I have up-and-coming trainers hit me up all the time and tell me they want to do exactly what I do for a living. They tell me they want to train the best players in the world, make millions of dollars, and travel the world running events. While I love my job and the fact that they want to follow in my footsteps, I make sure they understand all of the sacrifices that come with this type of life.

Most of them only see all the blessings and none of the burdens. They don't see the two-hundred-plus nights a year that I spend in a hotel room, which is a huge upgrade from sleeping in parking lots, but a sacrifice, nonetheless. They don't see the all-nighters I pull, breaking down film or missing holidays with my family to be there for my clients. These people also don't see the days my videographer Sam Limon must remind me to eat because I've been too busy to set aside time and grab some food.

You better be prepared for *all* the parts of The Work you must put in and the corresponding sacrifices you'll make. You can't always see them when you begin. Just know this part of The Work is out there and is a hurdle you'll have to overcome if you want to reach your goals.

HATE ME NOW, THANK ME LATER

Hate me now, thank me later is a slogan I frequently use when working with a new client—a valuable lesson I gained from my experience as a high school player.

Even though my freshman year in high school was in 2005, I still remember numerous conversations with my mom suggesting that I should transfer schools because Coach Blossom was holding me back.

Despite being one of the most talented offensive players in the area, my lack of commitment on the defensive end resulted in me playing fewer minutes than I believed I deserved.

While I knew defense wasn't my strong suit, it often felt like I was the only player on the team with such a short leash that I would be subbed out for every defensive mistake.

It not only frustrated me but made me *hate* Coach Blossom.

On top of limiting my playing time during games, he also forced me to play all-time defense in practice every day. While all my teammates rotated between defense and offense in drills, I remained on defense the entire time.

Other coaches in the area were offering to build their programs around me if I transferred to their schools, but my mom wisely steered me away from the easy way out. She told me that if I wanted my situation to improve, I needed to focus on getting better at defense, which was the last thing I wanted to hear.

Putting my ego aside, I walked into Coach Blossom's office the next day before practice and asked what I needed to do to improve on the defensive end. He told me the first thing I needed to improve was my mindset, urging me to start taking pride in getting stops and embracing that aspect of the court. Additionally, he stressed the importance of hitting the weight room to improve my strength, given I was only 5'7" and 135 pounds at the time.

He also explained that his insistence on getting me to buy into defense was not only for the benefit of the team but also because he understood my strong desire to play college basketball. He knew how hard I worked and wanted to improve my chances of earning college scholarships however he could.

As I was walking out of his office, he said, "Just know, I'm harder on you than everyone else, because I believe in you more than everyone else. The second I stop coaching you is the second I stop caring about you."

The valuable lesson I learned that day was that great coaches prioritize what players *need* to do, rather than allowing them to do what they simply *want* to do.

> GREAT COACHES PRIORITIZE WHAT PLAYERS NEED TO DO, RATHER THAN ALLOWING THEM TO DO WHAT THEY SIMPLY WANT TO DO.

From that moment forward, I was committed to both ends of the floor.

Two summers later, I found myself matched up against Kendall Marshall, the top-ranked point guard committed to North Carolina, at the Nike Peach Jam. The tournament was considered the most prestigious high school event in the country, so hundreds of college coaches attended each game scouting potential recruits.

I had a solid game offensively, scoring 8 points on 3 of 5 shooting and was 2 for 3 beyond the arc, but it was my defensive performance that caught the attention of many coaches in attendance. I held Marshall to just 3 points and he finished 1 for 11 from the field.

After the game, I received over a dozen new Division 1 scholarship offers, and among them was an offer from Belmont University, the school where I eventually played and graduated from.

Thankfully, Coach Blossom cared enough about my development to demand more from me on the defensive end, and good thing my mom didn't allow me to shy away from the challenge and take the easy way out.

Nowadays, I tell my clients that my job is to get them to do what they need to do, regardless if they want to do those things or not. Hence, the slogan. I don't care if they hate me throughout the entire process because I know they're going to thank me afterward when they see the results that The Work produces.

I constantly remind them that they don't have to love the process, but they must crave the results and trust that their hard work will pay off.

Here's the takeaway: When you crave the results so intensely, the work it takes to accomplish those results will become irrelevant. Deep down, when you want something bad enough, you will be willing to do whatever it takes. You will be willing to put in The Unseen Hours.

CONSISTENCY TRUMPS INTENSITY

Intensity is good. Consistency is better. If you are ridiculously faithful to the small things, you'll eventually get the big things that you are after. The little things are rarely little. Little things done consistently over time become big things.

> IF YOU ARE RIDICULOUSLY FAITHFUL TO THE SMALL THINGS, YOU'LL EVENTUALLY GET THE BIG THINGS THAT YOU ARE AFTER.

You may not think that little things add up, but they do. Eating a single salad won't make you skinny, just like eating an entire pizza won't make you fat. However, if you consistently eat more of one way than another, you'll notice a big difference in your body. Taking your son or daughter to the batting cages once or twice won't make them better ballplayers, but dropping hundreds of tokens into pitching machines over several years may just help them land a starting position on their high school team and perhaps even lead to scholarship offers.

While most of us want instant results, the real goal should be permanent results. The only way to get there is through consistent work.

Where most people go wrong is they end up burning themselves out trying to make intense changes that aren't sustainable over time. This is why I stress Micro-Shifts. They are attainable and become new baseline habits that you build on. You're growing over time as you build these new habits but you're doing it in such a way that you are energizing yourself instead of draining yourself because you've taken on too much.

For instance, some people say they want to get back in shape, so they head to the gym and go through an intense workout. Maybe they go back to the gym the next day, but after another day or two, most wake up sore and drained, and have no energy or desire to go to the gym.

After skipping one day of workouts, they end up skipping another and before you know it, they stop going to the gym altogether.

Sound familiar?

Or how about the intense binge diets that tell you to fast most of the day then avoid all your favorite foods? While the calorie deficit may help you shed a few pounds, almost everyone that tries them eventually goes back to their old eating habits because these radical changes are not sustainable.

Although intense changes may work for some, they rarely work for most. The key is making changes that you will stick with long enough and consistently enough for real change to occur. To avoid this mistake, don't ask what the most intense change is you can make. Instead, ask what is the most beneficial change you can make that you will consistently stick with. This is one of the pieces you'll need to get you on the right path to lasting change.

The other thing is that when you're thinking about The Change you want to make, be sure you can follow through not only on your best days, but on your worst days as well. That is a critical element of consistency. Design your MicroShifts with that in mind.

In fact, it's your worst days, not those days where you're in optimal flow, that matter the most. Too often, your plans are designed in your head's perfect world. The reality is you never live day-to-day in a perfect world. You will face new and often considerable challenges daily. You must factor in those challenges and still find a way to maintain consistency too.

In a perfect world, you jump out of bed and stick to your perfect morning routine, which consists of meditation, journaling, a workout, a cold shower, and a healthy breakfast. In reality, you stay bundled up under your covers for "just a few more minutes," scroll through social media way too long, smash your toe on the corner of your couch so that you can't focus on meditating and journaling, and grab coffee and a Pop-Tart before heading out the door.

While I'm all for having no Plan B and just making Plan A happen, allowing for a few hiccups along the way can be beneficial. There is an art to blending flexibility and consistency to work in your favor.

For instance, if you're planning to wake up early and cook a healthy breakfast every morning before work, having a few healthy grab-and-go options in your refrigerator could come in handy if something comes up in the morning and ruins your usual routine.

Likewise, if you're sticking to a specific monthly budget, setting aside funds for unexpected expenses could save you from a ton of unnecessary stress down the road.

DISCOMFORT OR PAIN

Every year, I see high school athletes cry when their seasons end after getting knocked out of their state playoffs. Losing sucks, but I only feel sorry for the players who did everything in their power to improve their chances of winning games.

If they weren't in the gym before school, lifting weights after practice, and studying film, they chose this pain. They could have chosen the sacrifice of working their butts off every day, but instead, they chose the pain of failure and regret.

The decision to choose between the discomfort of discipline and the pain of regret isn't limited to just athletes. It's true for all facets of life.

You can choose the sacrifice of working long hours to make and save money or the pain of feeling broke. You can choose the mental and physical discomfort of training for a triathlon versus the pain of feeling like you have not lived up to your potential by opting to relax and watch football with your friends each weekend instead.

Being disciplined can feel painful but it is nothing compared to the pain of regret.

THE NEXT PLAY MENTALITY

"Next play" is a well-known sports term that reminds players to play in the present and shift their focus to the next play instead of dwelling on past mistakes. Coaches know that when players dwell on one mistake, it often leads to another. When coaches drive this point home, it frees up players to forget the past so they can play at their highest level going forward. Carrying around past miscues in a game is the archenemy of the "next play" mentality. It's also why some teams lose consistently and why others rack up championships season after season.

It just so happens that my dad and I were in attendance for one of the most powerful examples of this during Super Bowl LI. The Atlanta Falcons scored four consecutive touchdowns to take a 28–3 lead midway through the third quarter. With 2:12 left in the third quarter, ESPN's win probability chart estimated Atlanta's chances of winning at 99.8 percent.

Much had gone wrong for the New England Patriots, but they chose not to dwell on their past mistakes. Instead, they kept their focus to the next play, enabling them to score twenty-five consecutive points and tie the game in the final seconds of regulation.

In overtime, New England won the coin toss, received the kickoff, and scored a touchdown, ultimately clinching their fifth title.

"Next play" isn't just limited to sports, it's great life advice as well.

Let's say you decide to go a month without drinking. The first couple days, you're locked in. Then, during a night out with your friends, they ask you to take a shot with them to celebrate someone's birthday. You rationalize that one shot is harmless. But after taking the shot, you realize you already broke the promise to yourself, so you might as well enjoy the rest of the night drinking with your friends and get back on track tomorrow.

Isn't it strange how often one shot leads to a night

full of drinking? When you wake up hungover the next morning, not only does your body feel like shit from all the alcohol, you feel like shit because you know you let yourself down.

It happens. It's another example of the real world intruding on the illusion of your perfect world. When something like this happens, the right thing to do is put it behind you. You can't change what happened. You can only learn from it. But you do have to learn from it! Then, move on to the "next play."

We are not born perfect, nor do we live perfect lives. That's what makes life worth living. We're the sum of our imperfections, which keep us humble and our lives interesting.

When you don't make any sales at work on Monday, shake it off and forget about it. Shift your focus to bouncing back and closing a few deals on Tuesday. If you go 0 for 5 in your softball league game, let it go, work on your swing a bit, and get ready for the next at bat. Did you blow off going to church with your family on Sunday morning? Ask for a little forgiveness and make sure you go to next week's services.

Erase the past if you haven't put full effort into what you wanted to accomplish. You can't change it. Dwelling on it only makes things worse. Accept that you're human, and by definition, humans are wired to make mistakes on a regular basis.

Just don't compound your mistakes and let them become bad habits that work against you. Do not let one mistake become two, three, or more.

Before you move on, give some intentional thought as to why and how those mistakes happened and what you can learn from them, so you don't repeat them in the future. After that, be kind and forgive yourself.

Then dig in and start again.

BOUNCE BACK BETTER

Embracing a "next play" mindset encourages moving past errors, but it is equally crucial to bouncing back effectively after moments of disappointment.

Every year, NBA fans debate which players should earn a trip to the NBA All-Star Game. Only twelve players from each conference are awarded this honor, so there are plenty of good players who just miss the cut each year.

After the selections were announced during the 2019–20 season, there was one name mentioned on every NBA All-Star snubs list: Brad Beal.

Beal's omission surprised a lot of people because he was averaging 29.1 points per game entering All-Star weekend, which was the most ever by a player who was not named an All-Star.

While Beal was disappointed as well, he couldn't

change the voting, so instead of dwelling on a result that was out of his control, he poured all his energy into making a statement on the court, which was something in his control.

He turned his game up to an entire new level.

In his second and third games back after the All-Star break, Beal became just the sixth NBA player to score 50-plus points on consecutive nights, scoring 53 and 55 points. He kept his scoring surge rolling and averaged 36.5 points per game the rest of the season, which helped him surpass his 30-point-average goal he set in the summer.

Brad didn't want to feel the same pain of being close but just short the following season. He's always been a relentless worker but attacked that summer with extra motivation and wanted to make sure he didn't give them a choice to leave him off the All-Star team the following season.

His hard work paid off, as he led the league in scoring entering All-Star weekend, which helped him finish first in fan voting, first in player voting, and first in media voting. Brad was voted to his third All-Star Game and selected as a starter for the first time.

Think of a time in your life when you fell just short of achieving a goal you set for yourself or were frustrated with a result that was out of your control. How did you respond? Did you feel defeated and give up or did you lace up your shoes and get back to work?

KEEPING PROMISES WITH YOURSELF

When others break their promises to us, we get upset at them. But when we break promises to ourselves, we often give ourselves a pass. You wouldn't want your partner to be "relatively" faithful to you, so why is it that you're okay with being relatively faithful to that big goal you set for yourself?

If you want to make improvements in your life, you need to start holding yourself accountable for the promises you make with yourself. Just as important, stop making promises that you're only going to honor if they're convenient to keep. Legitimate promises are commitments, not wishful hopes and "someday" dreams.

> STOP MAKING PROMISES THAT YOU'RE ONLY GOING TO HONOR IF THEY'RE CONVENIENT TO KEEP.

The problem with bending, breaking, and ignoring promises to yourself is that, eventually, you're going to stop trusting yourself. That lack of accountability creates an ongoing disconnect between what you say you're going to do and what you actually end up doing. When you stop trusting yourself, you leave the door wide open for the bullshit of self-doubt to creep in and take over.

On the flip side, when you keep promises to yourself, you build trust and confidence. These are essential building blocks you need to start accomplishing the goals you've set.

One of the reasons why I have so much self-confidence is because I've proven time and time again that I will keep the promises I make to myself. My superpower might surprise you: it's my sobriety. When I was in high school, I made a promise to myself that I wasn't going to drink, smoke, or do any drugs. Peer pressure is intense in high school, college, and beyond, but I didn't waver. I made a promise to myself, and I kept it.

Resisting temptation can be incredibly challenging if you're not fully committed and disciplined. But I was both, so it was easy. Even one drop of alcohol meant that I would have broken a promise I made to myself. It wouldn't have been the alcohol that caused the damage in this case. One sip surely wouldn't have even gotten me tipsy. But the disappointment from knowing I didn't have the discipline to follow through would have crushed me.

A few years back, I went clubbing in Las Vegas with a few of my friends and one of the players I coach. He found out about my sobriety pledge and was blown away by it. Then he tested me by offering me $10,000 to take one shot of vodka.

You may think I'm crazy or stupid, but I turned him down. I stuck to my principles and the standard I had set for myself, which is worth more than any amount of money. That continues to be the case to this day. As I write this, I'm thirty-four years old, and I have never tasted one sip of alcohol, never smoked, and never done any kind of drug.

This wasn't the first big promise I kept with myself. When I was twelve, I successfully challenged myself to not eat sweets for a month. Then I promised myself to not eat sweets for the rest of my playing career because I thought it would improve my body and athleticism. This meant no soda, no ice cream, candy, or cookies. Not one sip or one bite, even at birthdays, holiday gatherings, or hanging out with friends, when temptation is at its highest point.

I'd be lying if I said I didn't crave sweets plenty of times along the way, but I'd made a promise to myself. I wasn't going to break it. And I did not. I'm proud that I went more than ten years without eating any sweets.

No one else would have known if I occasionally cheated, but *I* would have. That level of discipline and the fact that I made a challenging promise to myself were what mattered most to me, more than a few Oreos, a Coke, a Twix, or a warm brownie with some vanilla ice cream on top.

When you can't keep promises to yourself, you're bullshitting yourself.

Do challenges like this take work? Of course they do! However, you'll reap benefits in ways you never could have imagined when you do keep promises to yourself. You can't see them when you start. Use that faith and those yet-to-be-realized benefits as part of the inspiration you need to see you through, especially when you start to waver.

By not taking a shot of booze for $10,000 and swearing off sweets for a decade, I chose discipline over dopamine. I made promises and firmly decided that nothing would derail me because I wanted all the benefits I could see and those that I couldn't that were waiting for me as part of that journey.

Make promises to yourself and keep them. Change is hard but if you can't do this type of difficult work, you may need to revisit how badly you want the change you're looking for and adjust to something more modest. You can always adjust the level of difficulty upward later. But don't shy away from the process completely, or you won't accomplish a damn thing.

YOU ARE A FLEXITARIAN

Two friends and I went to dinner after a Clippers game one night. I asked if either of them had any dietary restrictions before we picked a restaurant. One said she was a vegetarian, so we picked a spot with plenty of options for her.

When we sat down at our table, the waitress asked if we wanted any drinks or appetizers. All of us ordered our drinks then my supposedly vegetarian friend said, "If y'all want to share some appetizers, I say we get the sweet chili garlic boneless wings and an order of the grilled Korean barbecue beef."

The other girl and I thought she was joking, so we started laughing. But she wasn't. After a good laugh, we both looked at her and said, "We thought you were a vegetarian."

She smiled and said, "I am . . . but I'm flexible."

Being the smart-ass that I am, I quickly responded, "Sounds like you're more of a flexitarian."

I didn't know that "flexitarian" was a real thing, but apparently it is. By definition, a flexitarian is a person who primarily eats vegetables but occasionally eats meat. Sounds like a lot of people are flexitarians.

She laughed and tried to rationalize it by explaining that she only eats meat when she's drunk, which she was after enjoying several drinks at the game. I gave her shit and reminded her that vegetarians don't eat meat, regardless of how much alcohol they drink.

Many of us are like flexitarians in different parts of our lives. When we want to say we're this or that, but we pick and choose when we're this or that, it means we're really not that something at all.

You aren't a hard worker if you only work hard on the days you feel motivated. You aren't a tidy person if the only time you clean your house is when you're expecting guests. And you aren't a vegetarian if you eat sweet chili garlic boneless wings and grilled Korean barbecue beef when you get drunk.

If you want better results, go all in, all the time. Either you're committed to your success or you're not. There's virtually no middle ground where you can stand and defend your lack of commitment. As I've mentioned, when you do falter, and as long as it's only on rare occasions, don't beat yourself up. Start over again, but with deeper resolve.

Truthfully, it's easier to be all in than almost all in. 100 percent is easier than 90 percent. Let me explain.

100% IS EASIER THAN 90%

Let's say the change you want to make is to cut way back on your drinking.

You go out with your friends for happy hour and now you start getting tested. Peer pressure is always a challenge. Is tonight the night you're going to drink? If you drink, are you going to have just one or a couple?

There is nothing definite about what limiting your drinking means, so your friends know there is a chance you'll have a drink with them. As a result, they pressure you and make you feel bad for not having fun with them until you finally cave in. Having a drink is not on them. It's on you because you built in wiggle room to your commitment.

But what happens when you say you're going to stay sober for ninety days with no exceptions?

This time, when you go out with your friends, there is nothing to think about. It's black-and-white. No gray. You're all in. You know the outcome before you ever connect with your friends. You aren't drinking tonight or any other night for your ninety-day commitment. Your friends may still try to get you to drink, but after you put your foot down and let them know it's a hard "no" they'll eventually stop trying because they know you're not going to cave in.

That one concrete decision ends up making a ton of future decisions for you. And they're the right decisions based on the change and the work you want to put in.

The problem most people have is they paint white lines on the road instead of putting up concrete barriers. White lines encourage you not to cross them, while the concrete barriers ensure you don't cross them.

NO APPLAUSE NECESSARY

When you were growing up, your parents didn't stop at the door every morning and wait for a round of applause before heading to work. Why? Because they're supposed to go to work. It's what they do.

Too many people think they should be complimented for doing the things they should be doing as a normal part of living their lives.

Salespeople shouldn't expect a high five every time they make a sale. Athletes shouldn't expect a pat on the back every time they work out. And do I even need to mention what I think about participation trophies in youth sports?

Applause is external validation for an internal process of setting the bar high and going after your goal with everything you can bring to the effort. It's what you're supposed to do, and while a round of applause is nice when you reach important milestones or accomplish something hard, if that's why you're doing it, you're working with the wrong values and goals in mind.

As you might guess by now, you're also bullshitting yourself.

Do the work. Focus on why the work is important to you. Don't be distracted by the applause, and just as important, by the naysayers, because you'll have plenty of those too.

Find satisfaction, purpose, and motivation inside of you. Part of that means tuning out the noise. All forms of noise!

You might not get a big round of applause for doing the things you're supposed to do when you're working on your change. But you will love the results that those actions produce and that should mean more to you than any amount of validation from others.

FINISH THEM OFF!

There are few things more frustrating than when a main character in a movie knocks out the bad guy but doesn't finish them off. If you're like me when this happens, you probably yell at your TV and say "What an idiot!" because you know the bad guy is going to come back even bigger and badder than before.

Too often, we let bad habits linger, and just like bad guys in movies, the bad habits often come back to haunt us in the end.

If you want to be fit, you must kill off your unhealthy eating and sedentary habits, while also eliminating your negative thinking habits that blame your weight issues on factors like "big bones" or genetics.

You can't be financially stable until you kill off your bad spending and saving habits, impulse buys, and lack of budgeting because you're lazy.

When stress is eating you alive, find the sources of that stress, and take whatever steps are necessary to kill them off too. Your peace of mind means everything, and if you remove the bad relationship, crappy job, or sketchy neighborhood you live in, you're actively destroying critical parts of your life that are hurting you.

Bad habits may not screw you right now, but they will later. Just like overnight success doesn't really happen overnight, failure rarely happens by chopping your head off. Usually, it kills you with death by a thousand little paper cuts over time. Completely eliminating bad habits is the way to avoid those cuts.

> BAD HABITS MAY NOT SCREW YOU RIGHT NOW, BUT THEY WILL LATER.

Part of the work facing you is isolating these bad habits and applying focus and persistence until you finish them off completely.

UNBREAKABLE FAITH

The summer after my freshman year in high school, my sister and I played on AAU teams that went to Las Vegas to compete in a tournament. While we were there, one of my sister's teammates asked me about Isaiah Thomas, a high school player who was playing in the tournament as well. She said they were hanging out in the lobby, and he was bragging to her about how he was going to play in the NBA.

I started laughing. Although he was a really good player, Isaiah was probably 5'6" at the time. I told her that because of his height, he'd play college ball, but he would never make it to the NBA.

I was wrong. Not only did he make it to the NBA, Isaiah was named an NBA All-Star twice during his career, despite only growing to 5'9".

Like every kid that picks up a ball, I had dreams of one day playing in the NBA, but I thought it was impossible because of my height. Yet, I'm a few inches taller than Isaiah, and he made it. That's because Isaiah Thomas had something I did not.

Unbreakable faith.

He ignored the fact that the average height in the NBA is 6'7" and that there have only been about two dozen players in NBA history that were 5'9" or shorter. He tuned out the noise and remained true to his dream. And then he worked his ass off to turn it into a reality. What was impossible in the eyes of so many was completely possible in his eyes. And that's all that mattered.

That was a teachable moment for me. And it's one I'm reminded of every time I work with a CEO or a player. It also helped me understand the difference between asking questions about how to accomplish something and asking questions that are really barriers to what you want to accomplish.

It is the difference between asking "I'm 5'6" . . . what do I need to do to make it into the NBA one day?" and "I'm 5'6" . . . how the hell am I going to make the NBA?"

As I've already mentioned, the work you do must involve working on your mindset. Flooding your brain with positive and reinforcing messages can create an unbreakable faith in yourself too. The amount of mental intensity and focus you put into making a change usually determines how successful you will be in achieving it.

Unbreakable faith sets a standard. It keeps you attached to your purpose and your goal. That's critical to minimizing doubt, which is another bad habit that can fester and destroy your dreams.

Isaiah's journey and his unbreakable faith were incredible lessons for me and ones you can learn from too. Sometimes the things we deem impossible are, in fact, possible if we have the right mindset.

Never forget that!

RIDE THE WAVE

A few years ago, I tried surfing for the first time at Manhattan Beach. Keep in mind, I'm a Midwestern guy from St. Louis, and the only surfing I had ever seen before moving to Southern California was on YouTube.

As you might guess, my first attempts weren't pretty. So much so that while I was sitting on my board waiting for a swell, a local paddled over to me and asked, "You're not from around here, are you?" It was that obvious. He was cool about it, though, and gave me two pieces of advice:

> "When you spot a wave you want to ride, paddle your ass off if you want to catch it."

> "Once you catch the wave, you go where you look. If you look at the beach, you'll enjoy a nice ride to the beach. If you look at the rocks, you'll run right into them."

Those are great pieces of life advice as well. Find waves worth riding and put everything you have into getting the best ride possible. Also, stay focused when you're doing The Work, and chances are you'll enjoy the most exhilarating times of your life.

• • •

Life will throw a bunch of things at you, but the biggest challenges you'll ever face are the ones inside of you. They're constant and part of the price of being alive.

How you frame them is a big part of any change you seek out for a better life. That starts with a decision to either attack The Work in front of you or hide from those challenges and shrink into a life that's less than you deserve.

Settling is never the answer.

Do The Work.

THE REFINEMENT

The Work is critical, but it's also important to make sure The Work is working correctly.

In a perfect world, The Blueprint you designed would be perfect from the start. Unfortunately, we don't live in a perfect world, so you have to continuously audit what is and isn't working.

Inefficient effort produces inefficient results. When you're operating optimally, you'll get the best results.

I mentioned earlier that the best can always get better, meaning that there's always another level that you can reach for your health, business, relationships, financial situation, and so forth.

While The Blueprint focuses on what you can do before the fact, The Refinement focuses on what you should do after the fact. Armed with additional knowledge and experience you'll gain from your initial execution of The Blueprint, your refinement process is a key part of the overall "stop bullshitting yourself" process.

To refine our thoughts and actions related to The Change we want to make, we must relentlessly prioritize based on new information and input.

MY GRANDMA MIMI

I loved my grandma Mimi. We were beyond close for many years. But I still beat myself up to this day because the last conversation I had with her before she passed was on FaceTime. And it didn't need to be.

Several years ago, after being diagnosed with advanced-stage cancer, she was admitted to a St. Louis hospital, where I spent the next two days with her.

I left her side to go work out an NBA prospect for the weekend. I gave my grandma Mimi a big hug and kiss and told her that I was only going to be gone for a few days, and then I would be back by her side.

But the day before I came home, she passed away. I was sitting in my hotel room between workouts when I got the call from my mom. My stomach still turns thinking about it.

How dumb was I? I didn't get to see my grandma, whom I loved so much, one last time, despite knowing how sick she was. Instead, I spent her last few days in a gym, hundreds of miles away from where I should have been.

Damn, it's still one of the worst episodes of bullshitting myself that I've ever pulled, made even worse by how it impacted other people in my life.

I could have easily sent one of my other skills coaches to train the player or sent him a text with workouts to do on his own. I should have told him that I needed to be with my grandma, and he would have understood. But instead, I let something I deemed urgent steal my time from something that was genuinely important.

I learned the hard way that what's important is more important than what's urgent if what's urgent isn't as important.

I see many others make this same mistake. In The Blueprint, I defined a priority as *the thing* that is regarded as more important than any other. One thing.

That's why you circled The Change you wanted to make in The Blueprint.

Because if you aren't clear about your priority, life will pull you in a thousand directions. You'll try to be everything for everyone and leave nowhere near enough time for the single thing you've decided is most important.

I know that a lot of things feel important in your

life, but make sure you keep your main priority as your main priority. Don't learn this the hard way like I did.

RELENTLESSLY PRIORITIZE

Once you get clear on what's important, you need to ensure your life is reflecting that.

Before my grandma's passing, if you would have asked me what was most important to me, I would have answered without hesitation, "My family."

Yet, if you looked at my schedule, you'd see most of my time was spent on the road working out my clients, running events for players and coaches, or doing keynote speeches for businesses. In fact, the year my grandma passed, I slept in my own bed only twenty-two times. The rest of the nights I spent in a hotel.

It's easy to say something is your priority, but your actions define what your priority is.

Like many of you, I justified working my butt off as a way to provide for my family or get financial peace of mind for myself. That way, in my head, I didn't feel as bad when I was sending them gifts in the mail or wishing them happy birthday by phone instead of in person.

Yes, there are certain things you have to do to provide a comfortable living, but I've had dinner with billionaires who are frustrated by how little their family members appreciate them. At the same time, they don't understand the cause and effect that takes place because they can't take time off from their business ventures to spend time with their family, which is where the problem really lies.

That's one thing I respect most about my dad. As I was growing up, he worked grueling twelve-hour days most of the time. He made considerable sacrifices because he was providing for our family.

But he didn't use his long hours at work as an excuse to not be there for my sisters and me. He still volunteered as my baseball and football coach and didn't miss any of my basketball games.

When I wanted to get stronger, he took me to the gym before he went to work and taught me how to properly lift weights. And he still made time to take me to St. Louis Cardinals and St. Louis Rams games.

The point is that you can make competing parts of your life work in harmony. You can do all the things you must do and still have time for the things you want to do. It's not easy and you will need to compromise at times. But once you rank your life priorities, the decisions you make are much easier.

PROTECT YOUR PLATE AND YOUR TABLE

Tell the world you want to live a more meaningful life all you want, but if you keep saying "yes" to meaningless things, you'll never get to the place in life where you want to be.

You must be unmerciful when you prioritize the actions and activities that best serve you. Just as important, you must also be unmerciful when it comes to avoiding the ones that don't.

A common excuse people make about why they avoid change is that they are too busy. Being too busy is bullshit.

Being busy is usually a sign that you can't say "no" or that you don't have the focus, confidence, or clarity when it comes to the things that matter most. This results in you wasting time and energy on bullshit busyness to avoid or distract you from what you should be doing.

Your refinement process means placing a maximum value on your time, continuing to assess your priorities and the MicroShifts associated with them, and protecting your energy. Your gas tank is only so big, and you can only go so far, so battling energy vampires and time suckers by saying "no" must be a part of your future efforts.

You can't complain about having too much on your plate when the goal is to eat. But you can choose what to put on your plate and what you allow others to put on your plate.

It's like when you're at a family summer barbecue,

and all the cooks in the family have anted up their best dishes. Your mom makes her favorite potato salad and brownies, and others make sweet potato pie and slow-cooked baked beans with bacon, while your dad tends the smoker to ensure the rib meat is cooked until it easily falls off the bones. Just like life, the temptations are real and difficult to resist.

But when you're committed to eating healthy, if something ends up on your plate, it's because you put it on your plate or you let someone else put it there. You can still eat like a king or a queen with your aunt's green bean salad, load up on fresh fruits and veggies, and ask your dad to grill a couple of pieces of chicken.

This is a great metaphor for life. You must protect your plate if you want to protect your peace! To take it a step further, you also have to protect who you eat with because not everyone deserves a seat at your table. If they aren't bringing the right kind of food to your life, they shouldn't have a seat at your table.

For example, suppose you have a gambling buddy, and your friendship has always centered around betting on sports. When you give up gambling you must refine that friendship or not allow that person to have a seat at your table.

The most difficult form of refinement is elimination. If people aren't helping you grow, you need to let them go. When you stop wasting time with people who don't improve your life, you'll free up more time for the ones who do.

Unfortunately, a lot of people don't understand this or aren't willing to commit to the change they want to make in a big enough way. They surround themselves with clowns and then are surprised when their life becomes a circus.

As part of your refinement process, the next time you're stressing about being too busy, ask yourself if you're doing enough to protect your plate and your table.

TJ "ALL DAY"

TJ was my college roommate, but I decided to start calling him "All Day" after he declared he was going to give up sleep and work 24/7, because he was wasting too much of his life with his eyes closed. TJ made this decision because he read an article with alarming numbers on how most people waste their time.

He learned that in the course of a day, people spend about 6 hours working, 3 hours watching TV, 4 hours on the Internet, social media, texting, and on the phone, and just over an hour eating and drinking. That's about 14 hours a day, which means if you spend 9 hours sleeping and grooming, you have only an hour or so to devote to changing yourself. No wonder people say they have no time!

That next morning, I woke up early and saw that TJ was at his desk working. He'd worked through the night and did not sleep for a second, just like he said he would. He did the same thing the next night.

The following morning, I saw that TJ's door was closed. I knocked on the door and opened it. TJ was sleeping. In fact, TJ didn't leave his bed that entire day because he was sick. His plan backfired because he tried to cut out something that helped him instead of cutting out things that didn't.

One way to help understand what you need to keep doing and what you need to stop doing is by rewording The Change you want to make it into The Question.

For example, if The Change you want to make is that you want to make more sales at work, The Question is, "Will _____ help me make more sales?" When The Change you want to make is that you want to be healthier, The Question is, "Will _____ help me become healthier?"

This is how you don't fall into the same trap as "All Day" did. Things that help you need to earn a place in your life, and you can use this as the test to decide if they meet that standard.

"Will bingeing eight seasons of *Friends* help me

make more sales?" No. So don't do it. "Will stopping smoking or cutting way down on how much alcohol I drink make me healthier?" Yes! So stop engaging in those kinds of behaviors.

I wanted to get college scholarships when I was playing ball in high school. So, The Question for me was, "Will _____ help me get college scholarships?"

"Will waking up at 4:59 A.M. and shooting one thousand shots before school help me get college scholarships?" The answer was "yes," so I did it. "Will not eating sweets help me get college scholarships?" Improving your diet improves your performance. That was another "yes," so I did it. "Will drinking alcohol help me get college scholarships?" No. So I didn't do it.

There is no need to overcomplicate this exercise. Keep the questions and answers high level. Eventually, those high-level questions will drill down to smaller questions. But for now, get the big questions and answers right before moving on.

If you're serious about making The Change happen in your life, you will use The Question to optimize your life. As you continue to grow and your situation changes, The Questions should change as well. This is peak-level important in The Refinement process.

You must spend the majority of your time doing things that get you closer to making The Change a reality while avoiding the things that don't. Some parts of what you do to successfully complete The Change will remain constant. Others should face the scrutiny of unmerciful and constant refinement.

Stop right now and revisit The Change you said you wanted to make in The Blueprint. Then, to strengthen your resolve, ask The Question, or even better, ask several.

TO-DO AND NOT-TO-DO LISTS

We all know this line of Act 3 in *Hamlet*:

To be, or not to be, that is the question.

I'm going to remix Shakespeare and reshuffle The Question you must ask yourself.

To do, or not to do, that is The Question.

The Question is built on refining the things you should or should not do. That brings us to the next skill you need to master when prioritizing your life: creating your To-Do and Not-to-Do lists.

In The Blueprint, I mentioned most people have to-do lists so incredibly long that even on their best days and weeks they would have no chance at completing everything they want to do.

To avoid falling into that trap, I divide my To-Do List into three categories:

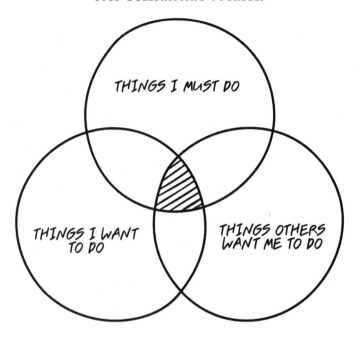

After I've done this, I prioritize my list to get to the most important things first. When you do this exercise, if you're struggling to identify what's most important, ask, "If I could do only one thing, which of these things would have the biggest impact?" It's pretty simple and highly effective, but some people can't figure this out because they're focusing on being busy and checking as many things as possible off their lists instead of the most important item.

Quantity is not a good measure of quality!

Also, remember this is a To-Do List, not a To-Do-If-It-Is-Easy-and-Convenient List. Regardless of how difficult or boring a task may be, if it needs to get done, get it done!

The other critical thing is to avoid multitasking. You'll wind up starting a bunch of stuff that will only distract you instead of letting you focus on the most important of all your To-Do List items. Do one thing. Devote full attention to it and then move on when you complete it.

After you prioritize the things you need to do, identify the things you're not going to do by creating a Not-to-Do List. This is just as important because it helps you think about all the distractions you might face going forward. If you can intentionally identify what these things are before you have to deal with them, it's easier to put them on a shelf, out of sight, where they belong.

To make your Not-to-Do List, ask, "What are the stupid and unnecessary things I do that are screwing up my life and getting in the way of what I want to accomplish?" Take as much time as you need. Build this list over days if that's what it takes. No item is too small to add. Keep in mind that a thousand small things can far surpass one big thing in many instances.

Most people only have To-Do Lists. By not understanding as fully as possible where resistance lives in opposition to what you want, you're only seeing half of the equation that you'll need to employ to solve the change you want to make. A Not-to-Do List means you can more fully refine and counterbalance your To-Do List so that both of these lists work in your favor.

TO-DO LIST:

- ☐ _____
- ☐ _____
- ☐ _____
- ☐ _____
- ☐ _____

NOT-TO-DO LIST:

- ☒ _____
- ☒ _____
- ☒ _____
- ☒ _____
- ☒ _____

PERSEVERE OR PIVOT

Sometimes, part of refining your process is quitting. At other times, you'll need to persevere and dig deeper to stay on course. The trick is knowing one from the other.

I know there are a lot of self-proclaimed gurus that tell everyone, "Don't quit!" In fact, when you type in "Don't Quit" on Google, it comes back at you with more than 1.5 billion results.

But there's no shame in quitting. Just the opposite. Pat yourself on the back when you quit things that are hurting you. I call this "positive quitting."

There are a lot of people who would improve their lives if they quit a shitty job, doing drugs, drinking, or an unhealthy relationship. Think of how much better your life would be if you could find the courage to quit bad habits and people who stress you out and add no meaning to your life.

The reason you must be laser-focused on quitting is that when you move out the junk in your life, by default you make time and energy for things that make your life better.

However, let's be very clear. You should only celebrate *positive quitting*—when you end something that doesn't benefit or serve you to make room for positive outcomes. You should never tolerate *negative quitting*—

giving in or giving up on things that do benefit you, which ultimately leads to negative outcomes. There is a big difference between the two and you must be completely honest why you're quitting something before you make that decision.

When you don't quit something that may be difficult but ultimately helps you, what you're doing is persevering. Perseverance is not giving up or giving in no matter what, regardless of how tough something is or what obstacles are in the way. There is nothing easy about making changes, so you need to be ready to persevere when times get tough. It's a test of courage and conviction.

The decision to make The Change is relatively easy when you create the right framework. Starting to put in The Work is challenging at first, but persevering long after the initial burst of motivation wears off is infinitely harder.

The most obvious example of this is New Year's resolutions.

In December, people tweet #NewYearNewMe. Then in January, you will see packed local fitness clubs with people who are excited about their new health journeys. But check back in March, and you'll see half-empty gyms with most of the resolute people nowhere to be seen.

They were so pumped about losing weight, looking good, and feeling better. They had a plan that they swore they were going to follow. They started putting in The Work, were on their way, and then . . .

Yep, you guessed it. They went back to their bullshit.

What happened? They will tell you that life got in the way. But the truth is, they got in their own way. Maybe they jumped on the scale or looked in the mirror and weren't getting results as quickly as they expected so they rationalized that working out was pointless. Or maybe they had a busy week at work, so they skipped a day, then skipped another, and before you know it, the habit of going to the gym had disappeared.

Whatever else happened, bullshit got the best of them. That can't happen if you want to become the best version of yourself! Your future self is relying on your current self to win your battles with bullshit.

Between quitting and persevering, there is a middle-ground solution. It is the pivot.

SMALL PIVOTS NOW LEAD TO MASSIVE CHANGES LATER

Joel Embiid is nicknamed "The Process" after famously saying, "You have to trust the process," in a postgame interview. While I love that line of thinking, I prefer the saying "Perfect your process." That's because when you perfect your process, you'll love what the process produces.

Pivoting is essential as you refine your approach, and perfecting your process is making sure you're constantly improving by making pivots. While there may be times when a massive pivot is required, often small pivots can lead to massive improvements.

For instance, the average person spends four hours a day on social media, texting, and emails. If you cut that number in half, you'd have an extra 730 hours a year of free time to work on that project you keep claiming you have no time for.

To tighten your finances, perhaps you decide to brew your own coffee in the morning instead of spending $6 on your favorite drink from Starbucks. Saving $6 doesn't seem like much, but if you do that for an entire year, you'll keep an extra $2,190 in your pocket.

Small pivots completed consistently over time lead to massive changes.

SMALL PIVOTS COMPLETED CONSISTENTLY OVER TIME LEAD TO MASSIVE CHANGES.

"Small pivots" is a misnomer because they're only small in the sense that you zero in on a single, individual act as part of an overall longer-term strategy. Small pivots completed consistently over time lead to massive changes.

Small changes are also easier to accomplish and over time, as they become new habits, you may lose sight of the fact that those longer-term results are what lead to large changes. Here's another thing that should excite you: when you make a small pivot in one area, and then save capacity to create small pivots in other areas, the cumulative effect of several small pivots is massive.

For example, the first time my sister Maddie baked me banana bread, it was good but not great. When I called to thank her, she asked how she could make it better, and I gave her some feedback. The next time she baked it, it was delicious. When I told her how much more I liked this second batch, she told me that she had only made a few small adjustments. A little less salt, a dash more sugar, and one more banana made all the difference in the world.

Pivoting is essential. In fact, you can pay a horrible price in the long run when you become rigid and don't grasp the importance of pivots in your life.

I've had four knee surgeries. I chalked this up to my intense work habits as a player and trainer. But my surgeon offered an additional reason. He agreed that the wear and tear was from the countless hours I spent on the court, but he said that one of the big reasons I put so much stress on my knees was a lack of flexibility in my back, hips, and ankles.

He said stretching and rolling out for as little as ten minutes a day when I was younger could have helped prevent some of these injuries. Damn, my dad was right. He always preached how important it was to stretch, but I ignored his advice because I didn't feel as if stretching for a few minutes a day would make a difference.

I was wrong. If I had pivoted early on and diligently took care of my body, I probably would have endured much less pain and fewer surgeries. I think about that a lot, which is why I'm so adamant about teaching that as a strategy now. All that pain I endured, and most likely for no good reason.

It was a tough lesson to learn.

ELEPHANTS, FLIES, AND FINGER TRAPS

Pivoting is essential, which I why I want you to lock in on this concept with three more of my favorite little pivot stories.

We'll start with baby elephants, who are often trained by attaching one of their front legs to a rope that is secured to a stake in the ground. Despite the young elephants' attempts to pull and tug and fight in order to free themselves, their size prevents them from breaking away from the rope. As a result, they soon realize that the rope is too strong for them to escape.

Once the elephants have been conditioned to think that the rope is unbreakable, zoo trainers can eventually take it away from the stake in the ground and lead the animals around. Despite being able to escape, the elephants never make any attempt to do so because they believe the rope is impossible to break. Their mind, not the rope, is what's holding them back.

Humans are the same way. We come to accept certain restrictions in our lives. What metaphorical ropes are restraining you? You have the ability to break free when you recognize that these ropes do not hold the power you believe they do.

Now go from one of the largest creatures on earth to one of the smallest. We've all seen a common housefly hopelessly attempting to escape to the outdoors by continuously buzzing and bashing into a window. Sadly, the fly's efforts are in vain, since it will never be strong enough to break the glass.

What the fly does not understand is that across the room, a mere twenty feet away, is a door that opens several times a day, providing the escape they so desperately seek. Despite this, the fly continues to try to find a way out through the window, and is doomed to die on a windowsill if it's not swatted first.

Just like a fly, many people are so focused on trying to break free from their current circumstances that they don't look for the door. Instead, they keep trying to break through the window, never realizing that a pivot in strategy could be far more beneficial. To find the freedom you want, you must adjust your current approach and do something that gives you a greater chance to succeed.

There is no better example of this than a Chinese finger trap. For those of you who have never played with them, a Chinese finger trap is a small hollow tube woven from bamboo. The bamboo means the trap is flexible, and the holes on both ends are just big enough for you to slip your index fingers in on either side.

It's easy to put your fingers into the trap, but when you try to pull both fingers out of the trap at the same time, the bamboo tightens and cinches down on them. The harder you pull, the tighter the trap becomes, making it even harder to escape. The key to freeing your fingers is to pivot from pulling your fingers to pushing the trap together, which increases the size of the tube and makes it easy to release your fingers.

Similar to a Chinese finger trap, sometimes the harder a person tries to free themselves from their circumstances, the more trapped they become. They think they are improving their situation by applying more effort, but in reality, they're making it worse. It's not a lack of trying, it's that they are trying the wrong solution.

> SOMETIMES THE HARDER A PERSON TRIES TO FREE THEMSELVES FROM THEIR CIRCUMSTANCES, THE MORE TRAPPED THEY BECOME.

Until the elephant, the fly, or you and your fingers learn the value of pivoting, each will experience frustration, anger, despair, or give up completely, admitting defeat.

Pivoting requires understanding the situation, analyzing the problem, and then refining the approach to solve the immediate problem at hand.

WINNING HABITS

Challenges come and go, but the winning habits you put in place stay in place, which is why positive quitting and pivoting are powerful ways to make lasting changes in your life.

When my younger sister Ashley was eleven, she had already reached Level 10 in gymnastics, the highest level in the USA Gymnastics Junior Olympic Program.

Since there were no higher levels for her to aim for, she faced the tough decision of either moving out of state to a Junior Olympic training facility or quitting the sport altogether.

Ultimately, she chose to leave gymnastics and focus on basketball, a sport she had only occasionally played as a child. While basketball was fairly new to her, she was no stranger to the required effort and commitment it took to excel at a sport after training for thirty hours a week in gymnastics.

Applying the same dedication she had given to gymnastics, Ashley, who was a year younger than me, decided to follow my intense training regime, working out with me every day. She began waking up at 4:59 A.M. to shoot one thousand shots before school, and then we would meet back at the gym after school to complete another skills workout.

That hard work paid off. Just three years later, she started receiving Division 1 scholarship offers after becoming one of the best players in the state.

This is a different kind of pivoting but just as essential to understand. The habits you create in one area of your life will stay with you as you take on new challenges in other areas. When you imprint the right kind of thinking and dedication, that habit stays with you, often for the rest of your life.

SIMPLEXITY

Refining is about removing impurities and improving clarity. The best way to do that is by simplifying your process.

Complexity is one of the great enemies of execution. Complexity kills your ability to get shit done. It paralyzes you by giving you too many choices and too many things to think about.

If you get overwhelmed by a Cheesecake Factory menu, you better believe you'll get overwhelmed by a complex blueprint that will lead you down a path filled with complex changes.

This is why you need to strive for *simplexity*. Simplexity means removing useless information, people, and habits from your life so you can focus on the best of the best. Without the burden of having an overwhelming number of choices to make, you can more easily engage in strategies and tactics that will lead to quicker results. Simplexity carves out the useless fat so that you can more easily build momentum.

When something is easier to do without sacrificing your bigger goal, you're more likely to do it.

THE STORY

A woman diagnosed with a terminal illness and given three months to live requested something unique from her pastor: to be buried holding a fork in her right hand.

When the pastor inquired about the meaning behind the request, she explained that when she was a child at family dinners, as everyone finished with the main course and dishes were being cleared, someone would always say "Keep your fork!" to signify that dessert was on the way.

She told the pastor, "When everyone sees me with a fork in my hand, they will surely ask, 'Why is she holding a fork?'

"I want you to tell them, 'It was her final wish for all of you to keep your fork . . . because the best is yet to come.'"

Apply this thinking to your life. No matter what you have been through in the past, you have the power to create a better future. Your best is yet to come if you decide to put your best foot forward from this day on.

Everyone gets to decide the life story they want to write. What will be yours?

WRITING YOUR STORY

I've shared several stories about me and others who have changed their lives when they stopped bullshitting themselves. But this book isn't about us. It's about you. That brings us to the last story. The most important story.

Your story.

Reading about how other people overcame the bullshit in their lives can be inspiring, but ultimately it is your story that matters most. Regardless if you're thirteen or sixty-five, single or have a big family, living on top of the world or if it feels like the world's on top of you, you have the power to change your story.

Understand that *nobody but you* gets to write your story.

When you first started reading this book, that may have intimidated or terrified you. If you've done The Work and paid attention to the strategies, processes, and standards I've laid out, you should now be energized by what comes next.

If you're not, that's okay. It just means you've still got some bullshit to overcome. It takes a lot of time and commitment. Give yourself credit, though, because reading this book means you've already started writing your new story. Build on that accomplishment.

Early on, I said this book was for people "who want a system to improve their lives by eliminating and defeating the bullshit that has always held them back."

You now have a strategic system that you can use to stop bullshitting yourself.

AUDIT YOUR **BULLSHIT**.
IDENTIFY **THE GAPS**.
MAKE **THE DECISION**.
BUILD **THE BLUEPRINT**.
PUT IN **THE WORK**.
REFINE YOUR PROCESS.
WRITE YOUR **STORY**.

The Audit helps you recognize all of **The Bullshit** that has caused you to settle and accept less than you deserve for too long.

The Gap is essential because you become aware of the differences between what you're doing now and what you need to do in the future to move to your desired outcome.

The Decision is the "flip the switch" moment that moves you from thinking about making a change to fully committing to doing whatever it takes to make that change happen.

The Blueprint is a detailed plan of action to execute The Change you want to make.

The Work outlines the steps and strategies you need to take to implement The Change.

The Refinement directs you to continually assess, adjust, and optimize your process to get the best results.

The Story is yours to write, and the outcome is entirely up to you.

ELIMINATING YOUR BULLSHIT

The only effective way to stop bullshitting yourself is to think of it as an ongoing process and not a project with clearly defined start and end points.

There is no single solution that will solve all your problems. Some form of bullshit will always be present.

Your ability and level of desire to identify, work through, and solve these challenges determines the amount of bullshit you'll tolerate versus the amount of peace, happiness, and success you'll find when you take matters into your own hands.

I have used the techniques in this book for several years now. As a result, you might think that I've filtered out all of the bullshit from my own life. In some ways I have, but in other ways, I'm still a work in progress.

We all are.

Whether we're an NBA superstar, a recent college grad starting on the bottom rung of the corporate ladder, a parent struggling to make ends meet, or facing health or relationship challenges, what separates us is much less than what binds us. No matter who you are or how you're writing your story, keep that in mind.

The vast majority of us have let external factors determine the course of our lives instead of taking control and choosing how we want our story to be written. We have allowed other people, events, and circumstances to shape our lives, instead of taking deliberate action to write it the way we want it to read. These are the chapters everyone has in the story of their lives, but that nobody wants to read out loud.

Some of us are so paralyzed by fear of the future and the bad outcomes of the past that we never dare to try to write a better story. You need to end that kind of bullshit thinking.

Start on page one if you must but make today the day that you start writing. None of us knows how our story ends, but when you stop bullshitting yourself, you will write a story you can be proud of for the rest of your life.

Everything you've ever wanted is on the other side of bullshit.

You have the system. You know what to do and how to do it.

There's only one thing left to do.

Stop bullshitting yourself.

SPECIAL THANKS

Madre: You truly embody the Mama Mentality. You never take a day off, never make excuses, and are always there for anyone who needs you, especially the girls and me—all while somehow managing to do it with a smile on your face. You truly are the most selfless person I know, and we're blessed to have you as our mom.

Pops: Seeing you work tirelessly every day to provide for our family, while always being there for us and never missing a game, didn't go unnoticed. You proudly bragged about us to every customer who walked into your shop, but know that we were just as proud to have you as our dad.

Ashley, Maddie, and **Lulu**: Y'all are the best siblings a big brother could ask for. Shley and Maddie, I apologize in advance if your kids start using the word *bullshitting*.

Papa Dink, Grandma Lee, Mimi, and **Papa**: Thanks for being the most loving and supportive grandparents.

Christine: I couldn't ask for a more perfect partner. You were the first person I shared a rough draft with, and you've patiently put up with me asking you to drop everything you're doing at any given moment to give me your opinion on just about every part of the book. Thank you for being you. I love you.

Bret Colson: Thank you for dealing with my nonstop texts, emails, and calls at all hours. I truly appreciate all your help throughout the writing process. Together, we've transformed 100,000 words into a book that I'm confident will help many people achieve their goals. Best idea wins!

Joel Embiid and **Jayson Tatum**: Having the backing of two of the best players in the world means a lot to me. A champ, an MVP, and much more to come for both of you. Appreciate y'all for trusting and believing in me throughout your careers, and know I'll be in your corners for life.

Aunt Janie: I've given you trouble for years about your birthday presents to me getting lost in the mail, but you more than made up for it with all your help on this book. Thanks for keeping it real and helping me dial back where I was a bit too blunt. This book wouldn't be what it is without your help and feedback.

Nick Amphlett: You believed in this book from the jump, and I can't thank you enough for your contributions and refinements that greatly enhanced the book. You said the Celtics were going to win it all and this was going to be a bestseller. Let's make it 2/2.

Raj Bhullar: The graphic guru did it again! Appreciate all the time and energy you spent on the artwork in this book.

Haley Heidemann and **WME Books**: Thank you for being the best book agents in the industry.

Andrew Yackira and **HarperCollins**: Thank you for bringing this book to life throughout the publishing process.

A huge thanks to all my friends who took the time to read through the book and share invaluable feedback during the writing process. I'd like to give a special shoutout to **Mike Whittier, Matt Hearty, Sam Limon, Karl Gokenbach, Francis Slay, Joshua Medcalf, Ben Newman, "Skeef" Keefer, Natalie Martin, Celeste Durve, Olivia Davis, Ben Bruno, Charlie Rocket, Rich Czeslawski, Kyle Gilreath**, and **Rap Brown** for letting me bounce ideas off them.

And finally, **THANK YOU!** Time is one of the most valuable resources in life, and the fact that you chose to spend your time reading this book means the world to me. I hope you enjoyed the stories and lessons and have begun implementing the systems and strategies to enhance your life. Few things bring me more joy than helping others achieve their goals, and I'm excited to hear about the improvements you've made in your personal and professional life using the system shared in this book. If I can be of any assistance to you, or if you'd like to share how this book is helping you, please feel free to contact me at drew@stopbullshittingyourself.com.